"A YOUNG MAN OR WOMAN DISCERNING A VOCATION MUST BEGIN by responding to a call to conversion and discipleship. It all begins with an awareness that Christ has cast his loving gaze on us and is calling us to a change of heart, to friendship with him. When Jesus invites the rich young man in the gospel, he wants the man's response to begin with an act of mercy, liberating himself from his attachment to money and giving that money to the poor. The young man is incapable of doing that because he does not begin to suspect how much the Lord loves him. Mark's gospel says Jesus looked upon him with love, but he was oblivious, he saw only his bank accounts and so he went away sad. Many people turn their back on a vocation because they are unaware of how much they are loved. In a time when young people are searching to discover God's loving mercy in their lives and his plan for them, Pope Benedict XVI's wisdom is a much-needed guide. I pray that this volume will give young people the strength and courage to answer the call to follow Jesus in a radical form of discipleship and ministry."

—*Cardinal Séan O'Malley, OFM Cap., Archbishop of Boston*

"AS A THEOLOGIAN, PRIEST, BISHOP, AND POPE, JOSEPH RATZINGER (Benedict XVI) ranks among the most gifted, fertile Catholic minds of the past century. *Called to Holiness* is a superb collection of his thoughts, both rich and accessible, on the meaning of the priestly and consecrated vocations. I warmly recommend it."

—*Charles J. Chaput, OFM Cap., Archbishop of Philadelphia*

"ONE OF POPE BENEDICT XVI'S GREATEST GIFTS TO THE CHURCH was his ability to communicate the richness and complexity of the living tradition in a way accessible and engaging for contemporary believers. Father Rossotti has brought together in one volume some of the pope emeritus' most insightful reflections on priestly and religious life. Seminarians and those in formation for consecrated life

will find in these pages much fruit for their own reflection and meditation. Priests and vowed religious, too, will benefit from having in one volume a compendium of homilies, talks, and addresses by Pope Benedict to deepen their own ongoing formation and renewal."

—*Most Reverend Kevin C. Rhoades, Bishop of Fort Wayne–*
South Bend

"FR. ROSSOTTI HAS USED BOTH HIS KEEN INTELLECT AND HIS compassionate heart to arrange the sublime words of Pope Emeritus Benedict XVI that provide seminarians, priests and all those interested in the Catholic priesthood with a coherent and systematic presentation of the very essence of what seminary formation really means—a call to holiness. As I read the pope's words, I was drawn into the mystery of the priesthood, which I try to live each day. I was so inspired by the pope's words that I wanted immediately to convey his message—really the perennial message of the Church—about the glories of the priesthood. I cannot wait to buy a copy for every seminarian here at Mount St. Mary's Seminary."

—*Msgr. Andrew R. Baker, S.T.D., Rector, Mount St. Mary's Seminary,*
Emmitsburg, Md.

"THIS OUTSTANDING COLLECTION BRINGS TOGETHER BEAUTIFUL texts on a theme central to the lifework of Benedict XVI. Directed in a special way to seminarians, the talks speak to the heart of everyone seeking to live the call to holiness in the world. A book by which to remember this profound pontiff!"

—*David L. Schindler, Gagnon Professor of Fundamental Theology,*
Pontifical John Paul II Institute for Studies on Marriage and Family,
The Catholic University of America

CALLED TO
HOLINESS

BENEDICT XVI

CALLED TO HOLINESS

ON LOVE, VOCATION, AND FORMATION

Edited by Pietro Rossotti

THE CATHOLIC UNIVERSITY OF AMERICA PRESS

WASHINGTON, D.C.

The paper used in this publication meets the minimum requirements
of American National Standards for Information Science—Perma-
nence of Paper for Printed Library Materials, ANSI Z39.48-1984.

∞

Cataloging-in-Publication Data available from the
Library of Congress

ISBN 978-0-8132-2924-9

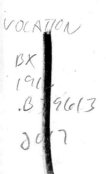

CONTENTS

CONTENTS

PREFACE

Pietro Rossotti

Throughout his papacy, His Holiness Benedict XVI always expressed deep love and care for seminarians. This collection of texts seeks to bring this concern to the public in an organic way, so that everyone in the Church, and outside the Church, can benefit from Benedict XVI's wisdom and teaching.

Presented here is a collection of the most relevant letters, speeches, homilies, and addresses of Benedict XVI to seminarians, men and women in consecrated life, along with his messages for the World Day of Vocations. The desire to collect these profound words of Benedict XVI comes from my experience as a priest involved in the formation of seminarians. The educational process of the seminary can be reduced to a period of training in order to acquire a set of skills apt to transmit a series of dogmatic propositions or, in the worst case, to implement new policies to run our parishes in more efficient ways. In other words, I see in myself, in other priests, and in seminarians that typical modern technological temptation to reduce our vocation to a worldly technique. Benedict XVI's words are so helpful precisely because they help us see the fallacy of this temptation, which the Holy Father often refers to as the temptation of activism.

Benedict XVI always brings us back to see things as they truly are. Such concern is particularly evident in his words to seminarians and people following the Lord in a life of total consecration. His primary aim is to help us see that vocation is a gift, and moreover, a gift of love. We cannot understand the meaning of priestly vocation, nor of any other vocation, outside of this more fundamental logic: man's life *is* relationship with God. Man does not find himself in front of an unknown God that remains hidden and careless, but the God of Jesus Christ, the God of love, the God who created us, who redeemed us, and who calls us to Himself. Therefore, according to Benedict XVI, to follow Christ in a life of complete consecration is very far from being an initiative of ours, an outcome of our moral and intellectual capacities. On the contrary, it simply means to follow, not without sacrifices and sufferings, the Lamb on the path He prepares little by little in front of us.

Thus, the period of seminary formation is of crucial importance in that it is the time in which we educate our whole life to simply be an answer to Christ, who continually calls men to Himself. We understand very well why according to Benedict XVI the seminary formation must be grounded upon silence, contemplation, study, prayer, and ultimately adoration of Christ. Indeed, how can anyone follow the voice of the beloved Christ without first listening to that same voice that resounds through the beauty of the tradition of the Church, the scriptures, the sacraments, and the community in which one lives?

Benedict XVI's words challenge us to realize that everything we do within seminary formation should be oriented toward a total openness and availability to Christ. Simply put, in the seminary we should learn to love in return the One who continuously gives Himself to us and for us. Upon such a foundation we can build a solid vocation, a vocation that does not collapse at the first moment of crisis. A vocation that is a real and reasonable sign of hope in our hopeless and unreasonable times of history assaulted by what Benedict XVI calls "a freedom without truth." Benedict XVI's words are words to be pondered and mediated on in silence. If we want to grow in holiness, we must embrace the sacrifice of listening to words that hurt our lukewarm heart, too often busy with unnecessary thoughts and worries.

I have divided these texts into three parts, inspired by the pope's Letter to Seminarians published in 2010, which I have selected to function as the introduction to this volume. The first part focuses on the mystery of vocation. In these texts Benedict XVI stresses the urgency to recuperate the original meaning of the word "vocation." The call to become priests, or to a life of total consecration to God, is a call to follow Christ and not a choice of the individual, even less a right. In the second part, I have collected Benedict XVI's words around the crucial experience of love, because ultimately to follow Christ is a journey of love. First, a journey into the love that God has for us, and following, a journey into our love for Him. The phenomenon of vocation is nothing else but this journey: a journey that makes our life blossom. In the third part, I have collected Benedict XVI's description of what a seminary should look like. Here, again, we should not expect any particular technique to build a better structure, but only words of wisdom, truth, and encouragement toward "building" saints. This trust in human freedom to respond to the gift of Christ brings about the hope that characterizes the address I have chosen as the conclusion to this book, the pope's 2013 reflections for the Pontifical Major Roman Seminary.

The texts of this collection are taken from the English texts on the Vatican website with only minor modification to aid the reader. In particular, greetings and concluding blessings in the spoken texts have been omitted, American spellings have been adopted, and citations have been moved to footnotes. The order and division of texts in parts is solely my responsibility, as Pope Benedict XVI never set out to produce such a collection. Without a doubt, he would have certainly done a much better job than I have. Although I attempted to avoid repetitions of themes, there is some overlapping. Last, I owe my gratitude to Marta Brown, who helped me with the editing of the volume.

I dedicate this small effort of mine to His Holiness Pope Emeritus Benedict XVI, with immense gratitude for his teaching and guidance, but especially for showing me who the priest truly is: *Alter Christus.*

CALLED TO
HOLINESS

INTRODUCTION

Men of God

From *Letter of His Holiness Benedict XVI to Seminarians,*
October 18, 2010

When in December 1944 I was drafted for military service, the company commander asked each of us what we planned to do in the future. I answered that I wanted to become a Catholic priest. The lieutenant replied, "Then you ought to look for something else. In the new Germany priests are no longer needed." I knew that this "new Germany" was already coming to an end and that, after the enormous devastation that that madness had brought upon the country, priests would be needed more than ever. Today the situation is completely changed. In different ways, though, many people nowadays also think that the Catholic priesthood is not a "job" for the future, but one that belongs more to the past. You, dear friends, have decided to enter the seminary and to prepare for priestly ministry in the Catholic Church in spite of such opinions and objections. You have done a good thing. Because people will always have need of God, even in an age marked by technical mastery of the world and globalization: they will always need the God who has revealed himself in Jesus Christ, the God who gathers us together in the universal Church in order to learn with him and through him life's true meaning and in order to uphold and apply the standards of true humanity. Where people no longer perceive God, life grows empty; nothing is ever enough. People then seek escape in euphoria and violence; these are the very things that increasingly threaten young people. God is alive. He has created every one of us, and he knows us all. He is so great that he has time for the little things in our lives: "Every hair of your head is numbered." God is alive, and he needs people to serve him and bring him to others. It does make sense to become a priest: the world needs priests, pastors, today, tomorrow, and always, until the end of time.

The seminary is a community journeying toward priestly ministry. I have said something very important here: one does not become a priest on one's own. The "community of disciples"— the fellowship of those who desire to serve the greater Church— is essential. In this letter I would like to point out—thinking back to my own time in the seminary—several elements that I consider important for these years of your journeying.

Anyone who wishes to become a priest must be first and foremost a "man of God," to use the expression of Saint Paul (1 Tm 6:11). For us God is not some abstract hypothesis; he is not some stranger who left the scene after the "big bang." God has revealed himself in Jesus Christ. In the face of Jesus Christ we see the face of God. In his words we hear God himself speaking to us. It follows that the most important thing in our path toward priesthood and during the whole of our priestly lives is our personal relationship with God in Jesus Christ. The priest is not the leader of a sort of association whose membership he tries to maintain and expand. He is God's messenger to his people. He wants to lead them to God and in this way to foster authentic communion between all men and women. That is why it is so important, dear friends, that you learn to live in constant intimacy with God. When the Lord tells us to "pray constantly," he is obviously not asking us to recite endless prayers, but urging us never to lose our inner closeness to God. Praying means growing in this intimacy. So it is important that our day should begin and end with prayer; that we listen to God as the Scriptures are read; that we share with him our desires and our hopes, our joys and our troubles, our failures and our thanks for all his blessings, and thus keep him ever before us as the point of reference for our lives. In this way we grow aware of our failings and learn to improve, but we also come to appreciate all the beauty and goodness that we daily take for granted, and so we grow in gratitude. With gratitude comes joy for the fact that God is close to us and that we can serve him.

For us God is not simply Word. In the sacraments he gives himself to us in person, through physical realities. At the heart of our relationship with God and our way of life is the Eucharist. Celebrating it devoutly, and thus encountering Christ personally, should be the center of all our days. In Saint Cyprian's interpretation of the Gospel prayer "Give us this day our daily bread," he says among other things that "our" bread—the bread that we receive as Christians in the Church—is the Eucharistic Lord himself. In this petition of the Our Father, then, we pray that he may daily give us "our" bread and that it may always nourish our lives; that the Risen Christ, who gives himself to us in the Eucharist, may truly shape the whole of our lives by the radiance of his divine love. The proper celebration of the Eucharist involves knowing, understanding, and loving the Church's liturgy in its concrete form. In the liturgy we pray with the faithful of every age—the past, the present, and the future are joined in one great chorus of prayer. As I can state from personal experience, it is inspiring to learn how it all developed, what a great experience of faith is reflected in the structure of the Mass, and how it has been shaped by the prayer of many generations.

The sacrament of Penance is also important. It teaches me to see myself as God sees me, and it forces me to be honest with myself. It leads me to humility. The Curé of Ars once said, "You think it makes no sense to be absolved today, because you know that tomorrow you will commit the same sins over again. Yet," he continues, "God instantly forgets tomorrow's sins in order to give you his grace today." Even when we have to struggle continually with the same failings, it is important to resist the coarsening of our souls and the indifference that would simply accept that this is the way we are. It is important to keep pressing forward, without scrupulosity, in the grateful awareness that God forgives us ever anew—yet also without the indifference that might lead us to abandon altogether the struggle for holiness and self-improvement. Moreover, by letting myself be forgiven, I learn to forgive others. In recognizing my own weakness, I grow more tolerant and understanding of the failings of my neighbor.

I urge you to retain an appreciation for popular piety, which is different in every culture yet always remains very similar, for the human heart is ultimately one and the same. Certainly, popular piety tends toward the irrational and can at times be somewhat superficial. Yet it would be quite wrong to dismiss it. Through that piety, the faith has entered human hearts and become part of the common patrimony of sentiments and customs, shaping the life and emotions of the community. Popular piety is thus one of the Church's great treasures. The faith has taken on flesh and blood. Certainly popular piety always needs to be purified and refocused, yet it is worthy of our love, and it truly makes us into the "People of God."

Above all, your time in the seminary is also a time of study. The Christian faith has an essentially rational and intellectual dimension. Were it to lack that dimension, it would not be itself. Paul speaks of a "standard of teaching" to which we were entrusted in Baptism (Rom 6:17). All of you know the words of Saint Peter which the medieval theologians saw as the justification for a rational and scientific theology: "Always be ready to make your defense to anyone who demands from you an 'accounting' (logos) for the hope that is in you" (1 Pt 3:15). Learning how to make such a defense is one of the primary responsibilities of your years in the seminary. I can only plead with you: be committed to your studies! Take advantage of your years of study! You will not regret it. Certainly, the subjects that you are studying can often seem far removed from the practice of the Christian life and the pastoral ministry. Yet it is completely mistaken to start questioning their practical value by asking, will this be helpful to me in the future? Will it be practically or pastorally useful? The point is not simply to learn evidently useful things, but to understand and appreciate the internal structure of the faith as a whole, so that it can become a response to people's questions, which on the surface change from one generation to another yet ultimately remain the same. For this reason it is important to move beyond the changing questions of the moment in order to grasp the real questions and so to understand how the answers are real answers. It is important to have a thorough knowledge of sacred Scripture as a whole, in its unity as the Old and the New Testaments: the shaping of texts, their literary characteristics, the process by which they came to form the canon of sacred books, their dynamic inner unity, a unity that may not be immediately apparent but that in fact gives the individual texts their full meaning. It is important to be familiar with the Fathers and the great Councils in which the Church appropriated, through faith-filled reflection, the essential statements of Scripture. I could easily go on. What we call dogmatic theology is the understanding of the individual contents of the faith in their unity, indeed, in their ultimate simplicity: each single element is, in the end, only an unfolding of our faith in the one God who has revealed himself to us and continues to do so. I do not need to point out the importance of knowing the essential issues of moral theology and Catholic social teaching. The importance nowadays of ecumenical theology, and of a knowledge of the different Christian communities, is obvious, as is the need for a basic introduction to the great religions, to say nothing of philosophy: the understanding of that human process of questioning and searching to which faith seeks to respond. But you should also learn to understand and—dare I say it—to love canon law, appreciating how necessary it is and valuing its practical applications: a society without law would be a society without rights. Law is the condition of love. I will not go on with this list, but I simply say once more: love the study of theology and carry it out in the clear realization that theology is anchored in the living community of the Church, which, with her authority, is not the antithesis of theological science but its presupposition. Cut off from the believing Church, theology would cease to be itself, and instead it would become a medley of different disciplines lacking inner unity.

Your years in the seminary should also be a time of growth toward human maturity. It is important for the priest, who is called to accompany others through the journey of life up to the threshold of death, to have the right balance of heart and mind, reason and feeling, body and soul, and to be humanly integrated. To the theological virtues the Christian tradition has always joined the cardinal virtues derived from human experience and philosophy and, more generally, from the sound ethical tradition of humanity. Paul makes this point very clearly to the Philippians: "Finally, brothers, whatever is true, whatever is honorable, whatever is just, whatever is pure, whatever is pleasing, whatever is commendable, if there is any excellence and if there is anything worthy of praise, think about these things" (Phil 4:8). This also involves the integration of sexuality into the whole personality. Sexuality is a gift of the Creator, yet it is also a task that relates to a person's growth toward human maturity. When it is not integrated within the person, sexuality becomes banal and destructive. Today we can see many examples of this in our society. Recently we have seen with great dismay that some priests disfigured their ministry by sexually abusing children and young people. Instead of guiding people to greater human maturity and setting them an example, their abusive behavior caused great damage for which we feel profound shame and regret. As a result of all this, many people, perhaps even some of you, might ask whether it is good to become a priest; whether the choice of celibacy makes any sense as a truly human way of life. Yet even the most reprehensible abuse cannot discredit the priestly mission, which remains great and pure. Thank God, all of us know exemplary priests, men shaped by their faith, who bear witness that one can attain to an authentic, pure, and mature humanity in this state and specifically in the life of celibacy. Admittedly, what has happened should make us all the more watchful and attentive, precisely in order to examine ourselves earnestly, before God, as we make our way toward priesthood, so as to understand whether this is his will for me. It is the responsibility of your confessor and your superiors to accompany you and help you along this path of discernment. It is an essential part of your journey to practice the fundamental human virtues, with your gaze fixed on the God who has revealed himself in Christ, and to let yourselves be purified by him ever anew.

The origins of a priestly vocation are nowadays more varied and disparate than in the past. Today the decision to become a priest often takes shape after one has already entered upon a secular profession. Often it grows within the Communities, particularly within the Movements, that favor a communal encounter with Christ and his Church, spiritual experiences and joy in the service of the faith. It also matures in very personal encounters with the nobility and the wretchedness of human existence. As a result, candidates for the priesthood often live on very different spiritual continents. It can be difficult to recognize the common elements of one's future mandate and its spiritual path. For this very reason, the seminary is important as a community that advances above and beyond differences of spirituality. The Movements are a magnificent thing. You know how much I esteem them and love them as a gift of the Holy Spirit to the Church. Yet they must be evaluated by their openness to what is truly Catholic, to the life of the whole Church of Christ, which for all her variety still remains one. The seminary is a time when you learn with one another and from one another. In community life, which can at times be difficult, you should learn generosity and tolerance, not only bearing with, but also enriching one another, so that each of you will be able to contribute his own gifts to the whole, even as all serve the same Church, the same Lord. This school of tolerance, indeed, of mutual acceptance and mutual understanding in the unity of Christ's Body, is an important part of your years in the seminary.

Dear seminarians, with these few lines I have wanted to let you know how often I think of you, especially in these difficult times, and how close I am to you in prayer. Please pray for me, that I may exercise my ministry well, as long as the Lord may wish. I entrust your journey of preparation for priesthood to the maternal protection of Mary Most Holy, whose home was a school of goodness and of grace. May Almighty God bless you all, the Father, the Son, and the Holy Spirit.

PART 1

THE MYSTERY OF
VOCATION

1. Called to Be Sons

From *Message of His Holiness Pope Benedict XVI for the 43rd World Day of Prayer for Vocations*, May 7, 2006

The celebration of the coming World Day of Prayer for Vocations gives me the opportunity to invite the entire People of God to reflect on the theme *Vocation in the mystery of the Church.* The Apostle Paul writes, "Blessed be the God and Father of our Lord Jesus Christ ... even as he chose us in him before the foundation of the world. ... He destined us in love to be his sons through Jesus Christ" (Eph 1:3–5). Before the creation of the world, before our coming into existence, the heavenly Father chose us personally, calling us to enter into a filial relationship with Him, through Jesus, the Incarnate Word, under the guidance of the Holy Spirit. Dying for us, Jesus introduced us into the mystery of the Father's love, a love that completely envelops his Son and that He offers to all of us. In this way, united with Jesus, the Head, we form a sole body, the Church.

The weight of two millennia of history makes it difficult to grasp the novelty of this captivating mystery of divine adoption, which is at the center of St. Paul's teaching. As the Apostle reminds us, the Father "has made known to us the mystery of his will ... as a plan to unite all things in him" (Eph 1:9–10). And he adds, with enthusiasm, "In everything God works for good with those who love him, who are called according to his purpose. For those whom he foreknew he also predestined to be conformed to the image of his Son, in order that he might be the first-born among many brethren" (Rom 8:28–29). The vision is indeed fascinating: we are called to live as brothers and sisters of Jesus, to feel that we are sons and daughters of the same Father. This is a gift that overturns every purely human idea and plan. The confession of the true faith opens wide our minds and hearts to the inexhaustible mystery of God, which permeates human existence. What should be said therefore of the temptation, which is very strong nowadays, to feel that we are self-sufficient to the point that we become closed to God's mysterious plan for each of us? The love of the Father, which is revealed in the person of Christ, puts this question to us.

In order to respond to the call of God and start on our journey, it is not necessary to be already perfect. We know that the prodigal son's awareness of his own sin allowed him to set out on his return journey and thus feel the joy of reconciliation with the Father. Weaknesses and human limitations do not present an obstacle, as long as they help make us more aware of the fact that we are in need of the redeeming grace of Christ. This is the experience of St. Paul, who confessed, "I will all the more gladly boast of my weaknesses, that the power of Christ may rest upon me" (2 Cor 12:9). In the mystery of the Church, the mystical Body of Christ, the divine power of love changes the heart of man, making him able to communicate the love of God to his brothers and sisters. Throughout the centuries many men and women, transformed by divine love, have consecrated their lives to the cause of the Kingdom. Already on the shores of the Sea of Galilee, many allowed themselves to be won by

Jesus: they were in search of healing in body or spirit, and they were touched by the power of his grace. Others were chosen personally by Him and became his apostles. We also find some, like Mary Magdalene and others, who followed him on their own initiative, simply out of love. Like the disciple John, they too found a special place in his heart. These men and women, who knew the mystery of the love of the Father through Jesus, represent the variety of vocations that have always been present in the Church. The model of one called to give witness in a particular manner to the love of God is Mary, the Mother of Jesus, who in her pilgrimage of faith is directly associated with the mystery of the Incarnation and Redemption.

In Christ, the Head of the Church, which is his Body, all Christians form "a chosen race, a royal priesthood, a holy nation, God's own people, that you may declare the wonderful deeds of him" (1 Pt 2:9). The Church is holy, even if her members need to be purified, in order that holiness, which is a gift of God, can shine forth from them with its full splendor. The Second Vatican Council highlights the universal call to holiness, when it affirms, "The followers of Christ are called by God, not because of their works, but according to his own purpose and grace. They are justified in the Lord Jesus, because in the Baptism of faith they truly become sons of God and sharers in the divine nature. In this way, they are really made holy."[1] Within the framework of this universal call, Christ, the High Priest, in his solicitude for the Church, calls persons in every generation who

---

1. Cf. Second Vatican Council, Dogmatic Constitution *Lumen Gentium* (November 21, 1964), no. 40.

are to care for his people. In particular, he calls to the ministeri-al priesthood men who are to exercise a fatherly role, the source of which is within the very fatherhood of God (cf. Eph 3:14). The mission of the priest in the Church is irreplaceable. Therefore, even if in some regions there is a scarcity of clergy, it should never be doubted that Christ continues to raise up men who, like the Apostles, leaving behind all other work, dedicate them-selves completely to the celebration of the sacred mysteries, to the preaching of the Gospel and to pastoral ministry. In the Ap-ostolic Exhortation *Pastores Dabo Vobis*, my venerable Predeces-sor Pope John Paul II wrote in this regard, "The relation of the priest to Jesus Christ, and in him to his Church, is found in the very being of the priest by virtue of his sacramental consecra-tion/anointing and in his activity, that is, in his mission or min-istry. In particular, 'the priest minister' is the servant of Christ present in the Church as *mystery, communion, and mission*. In vir-tue of his participation in the 'anointing' and 'mission' of Christ, the priest can continue Christ's prayer, word, sacrifice, and salv-ific action in the Church. In this way, the priest is a *servant of the Church as mystery* because he actuates the Church's sacramental signs of the presence of the risen Christ.'"[2]

Another special vocation, which occupies a place of honor in the Church, is the call to the consecrated life. Following the example of Mary of Bethany, who "sat at the Lord's feet and lis-tened to his teaching" (Lk 10:39), many men and women con-secrate themselves to a total and exclusive following of Christ. Although they undertake various services in the field of human

2. Pope John Paul II, Apostolic Exhortation *Pastores Dabo Vobis* (March 25, 1992), no. 16.

formation and care of the poor, in teaching or in assisting the sick, they do not consider these activities as the principal purpose of their life, since, as the Code of Canon Law well underlines, "the first and foremost duty of all religious is to be the contemplation of divine things and assiduous union with God in prayer."[3] Moreover, in the Apostolic Exhortation *Vita Consecrata*, Pope John Paul II noted, "In the Church's tradition religious profession is considered to be a special and fruitful deepening of the consecration received in Baptism, inasmuch as it is the means by which the close union with Christ already begun in Baptism develops in the gift of a fuller, more explicit, and authentic configuration to him through the profession of the evangelical counsels."[4]

Remembering the counsel of Jesus, "The harvest is plentiful, but the laborers are few; pray therefore the Lord of the harvest to send out laborers into his harvest" (Mt 9:37), we readily recognize the need to pray for vocations to the priesthood and to the consecrated life. It is not surprising that, where people pray fervently, vocations flourish. The holiness of the Church depends essentially on union with Christ and on being open to the mystery of grace that operates in the hearts of believers. Therefore, I invite all the faithful to nurture an intimate relationship with Christ, Teacher and Pastor of his people, by imitating Mary who kept the divine mysteries in her heart and pondered them constantly (cf. Lk 2:19). Together with her, who occupies a central position in the mystery of the Church, we pray:

3. Catholic Church, *Code of Canon Law: Latin-English Edition* (Washington, D.C.: Canon Law Society of America, 1983), canon 663, §1.
4. Pope John Paul II, Apostolic Exhortation *Vita Consecrata* (March 25, 1996), no. 30.

O Father, raise up among Christians
abundant and holy vocations to the priesthood,
who keep the faith alive
and guard the blessed memory of your Son Jesus
through the preaching of his word
and the administration of the Sacraments,
with which you continually renew your faithful.
Grant us holy ministers of your altar,
who are careful and fervent guardians of the Eucharist,
the sacrament of the supreme gift of Christ
for the redemption of the world.
Call ministers of your mercy,
who, through the sacrament of Reconciliation,
spread the joy of your forgiveness.
Grant, O Father, that the Church may welcome with joy
the numerous inspirations of the Spirit of your Son
and, docile to His teachings,
may she care for vocations to the ministerial priesthood
and to the consecrated life.
Sustain the Bishops, priests and deacons,
consecrated men and women, and all the baptized in Christ,
so that they may faithfully fulfill their mission
at the service of the Gospel.
This we pray through Christ our Lord. Amen.
Mary, Queen of Apostles, pray for us.

2. *A Mystery of Faith*

From *Address by the Holy Father, Encounter with Men and Women Religious, Seminarians, and Representatives of Ecclesial Movements,* Pastoral Visit of His Holiness Pope Benedict XVI to Poland, Czestochowa, May 26, 2006

Just as the Apostles together with Mary "went to the upper room" and there "with one accord devoted themselves to prayer" (Acts 1:12–14), so we too have come together today at Jasna Góra, which for us at this hour is the "upper room" where Mary, the Mother of the Lord, is among us. Today it is she who leads our meditation; she teaches us how to pray. Mary shows us how to open our minds and our hearts to the power of the Holy Spirit, who comes to us so as to be brought to the whole world.

My dear friends, we need a moment of silence and recollection to place ourselves in her school so that she may teach us how to live from faith, how to grow in faith, how to remain in contact with the mystery of God in the ordinary, everyday events of our lives. With feminine tact and with "the ability to combine penetrating intuition with words of support and encouragement,"[5] Mary sustained the faith of Peter and the Apostles in the Upper Room, and today she sustains my faith and your faith.

"Faith is contact with the mystery of God,"[6] to quote Pope John Paul II, because "to believe means 'to abandon oneself' to the truth of the word of the living God, knowing and hum-

---

5. Cf. Pope John Paul II, Encyclical Letter *Redemptoris Mater* (March 25, 1987), no. 46.
6. Ibid., no. 17.

bly recognizing 'how unsearchable are his judgments and how inscrutable his ways.'"[7] Faith is the gift, given to us in Baptism, which makes our encounter with God possible. God is hidden in mystery; to claim to understand him would mean to want to confine him within our thinking and knowing and consequently to lose him irremediably. With faith, however, we can open up a way through concepts, even theological concepts, and can "touch" the living God. And God, once touched, immediately gives us his power. When we abandon ourselves to the living God, when in humility of mind we have recourse to him, a kind of hidden stream of divine life pervades us. How important it is to believe in the power of faith, in its capacity to establish a close bond with the living God! We must give great attention to the development of our faith, so that it truly pervades all our attitudes, thoughts, actions, and intentions. Faith has a place, not only in our state of soul and religious experiences, but above all in thought and action, in everyday work, in the struggle against ourselves, in community life, and in the apostolate, because it ensures that our life is pervaded by the power of God himself. Faith can always bring us back to God even when our sin leads us astray.

In the Upper Room the Apostles did not know what awaited them. They were afraid and worried about their own future. They continued to marvel at the death and resurrection of Jesus and were in anguish at being left on their own after his ascension into Heaven. Mary, "she who believed in the fulfillment of the Lord's words" (cf. Lk 1:45), assiduous in prayer alongside the Apostles, taught perseverance in the faith. By her own attitude

7. Ibid., no. 14.

she convinced them that the Holy Spirit, in his wisdom, knew well the path on which he was leading them, and that consequently they could place their confidence in God, giving themselves to him unreservedly, with their talents, their limitations, and their future.

Many of you here present have experienced this secret call of the Holy Spirit and have responded with complete generosity of heart. The love of Jesus "poured into your hearts through the Holy Spirit who has been given to you" (cf. Rom 5:5), has shown you the way of the consecrated life. It was not you who looked for it. It was Jesus who called you, inviting you to a more profound union with him. In the sacrament of Holy Baptism you renounced Satan and his works and received the necessary graces for a Christian life and for holiness. From that moment the grace of faith has blossomed within you and has enabled you to be united with God. At the moment of your religious profession or promises, faith led you to a total adherence to the mystery of the Heart of Jesus, whose treasures you have discovered. You then renounced such good things as disposing freely of your life, having a family, acquiring possessions, so as to be free to give yourselves without reserve to Christ and to his Kingdom. Do you remember your enthusiasm when you began the pilgrimage of the consecrated life, trusting in the grace of God? Try not to lose this first fervor, and let Mary lead you to an ever fuller adherence. Dear men and women religious, dear consecrated persons! Whatever the mission entrusted to you, whatever cloistered or apostolic service you are engaged in, maintain in your hearts the primacy of your consecrated life. Let it renew your faith. The consecrated life, lived in faith, unites you closely to God, calls forth charisms, and confers an extraordinary fruitfulness to your service.

Dear candidates to the priesthood! So much can be gained by reflecting on the way Mary learned from Jesus! From her very first "fiat," through the long, ordinary years of the hidden life, as she brought up Jesus, or when at Cana in Galilee she asked for the first sign, or when finally on Calvary, by the Cross, she looked on Jesus, she "learned" him moment by moment. Firstly in faith and then in her womb, she received the Body of Jesus and then gave birth to him. Day after day, enraptured, she adored him. She served him with solicitous love, singing the *Magnificat* in her heart. On your journey of preparation, and in your future priestly ministry, let Mary guide you as you "learn" Jesus. Keep your eyes fixed on him. Let him form you, so that in your ministry you will be able to show him to all who approach you. When you take into your hands the Eucharistic Body of Jesus so as to nourish his People, and when you assume responsibility for that part of the Mystical Body that will be entrusted to you, remember the attitude of wonder and adoration that characterized Mary's faith. As she in her solicitous, maternal love for Jesus, preserved her virginal love filled with wonder, so also you, as you genuflect at the moment of consecration, preserve in your soul the ability to wonder and to adore. Know how to recognize in the People of God entrusted to you the signs of Christ's presence. Be mindful and attentive to the signs of holiness that God will show you among the faithful. Do not fear future duties or the unknown! Do not fear that words will fail you or that you will encounter rejection! The world and the Church need priests, holy priests.

Dear representatives of the new Movements in the Church, the vitality of your communities is a sign of the Holy Spirit's active presence! It is from the faith of the Church and from the richness of the fruits of the Holy Spirit that your mission has been born. My prayer is that you will grow ever more numerous so as to serve the cause of the Kingdom of God in today's world. Believe in the grace of God that accompanies you and bring it into the living fabric of the Church, especially in places the priest or religious cannot reach. The movements you belong to are many. You are nourished by different schools of spirituality recognized by the Church. Draw upon the wisdom of the saints, have recourse to the heritage they have left us. Form your minds and your hearts on the works of the great masters and witnesses of the faith, knowing that the schools of spirituality must not be a treasure locked up in monastic libraries. The Gospel wisdom, contained in the writings of the great saints and attested to in their lives, must be brought in a mature way, not childishly or aggressively, to the world of culture and work, to the world of the media and politics, to the world of family and social life. The authenticity of your faith and mission, which does not draw attention to itself but truly radiates faith and love, can be tested by measuring it against Mary's faith. Mirror yourselves in her heart. Remain in her school!

When the Apostles, filled with the Holy Spirit, went out to the whole world proclaiming the Gospel, one of them, John, the Apostle of love, took Mary into his home (cf. Jn 19:27). It was precisely because of his profound bond with Jesus and with Mary that he could so effectively insist on the truth that "God is love" (1 Jn 4:8, 16). These were the words that I placed at the beginning of the first Encyclical of my Pontificate: *Deus Caritas Est!* This is the most important, most central truth about God. To all for whom it is difficult to believe in God, I say again today, "God is love." Dear friends, be witnesses to this truth. You will surely be so if you place yourselves in the school of Mary. Beside her you will experience for yourselves that God is love, and you will transmit this message to the world with the richness and the variety that the Holy Spirit will know how to enkindle.

3. Do Not Be Afraid

From *Homily of the Holy Father, Marian Vespers with the Religious and Seminarians of Bavaria*, Apostolic Journey of His Holiness Benedict XVI to Munich, Altötting, and Regensburg, Basilica of Saint Anne, Altötting, September 11, 2006

Here in Altötting, in this grace-filled place, we have gathered—seminarians preparing for the priesthood, priests, men and women religious, and members of the Society for Spiritual Vocations—gathered in the Basilica of Saint Anne, before the shrine to her daughter, the Mother of the Lord. We have gathered here to consider our vocation to serve Jesus Christ and, under the watchful gaze of Saint Anne, in whose home the greatest vocation in the history of salvation developed, to understand it better. Mary received her vocation from the lips of an angel. The Angel does not enter our room visibly, but the Lord has a plan for each of us, he calls each one of us by name. Our task is to learn how to listen, to perceive his call, to be courageous and faithful in following him and, when all is said and done, to be found trustworthy servants who have used well the gifts given us.

We know that the Lord seeks laborers for his harvest. He himself said as much: "The harvest is plentiful, but the laborers are few; therefore ask the Lord of the harvest to send out laborers into his harvest" (Mt 9:37–38). That is why we are gathered here: to make this urgent request to the Lord of the harvest. God's harvest is indeed great, and it needs laborers: in the so-called Third World—in Latin America, in Africa, and in Asia—people are waiting for heralds to bring them the Gospel of peace, the good news of God who became man. But also in the so-called West, here among us in Germany, and in the vast lands of Russia it is true that a great harvest could be reaped. But there is a lack of people willing to become laborers for God's harvest. Today it is as then, when the Lord was moved with pity for the crowds that seemed like sheep without a shepherd—people who probably knew how to do many things, but found it hard to make sense of their lives. Lord, look upon our troubled times, which need preachers of the Gospel, witnesses to you, persons who can point the way toward "life in abundance!" Look upon our world and feel pity once more! Look upon our world and send us laborers! With this petition we knock on God's door; but with the same petition the Lord is also knocking on the doors of our own heart. Lord, do you want me? Is it not perhaps too big for me? Am I too small for this? "Do not be afraid," the Angel said to Mary. "Do not fear: I have called you by name" (Is 43:1), God says through the Prophet Isaiah to us— to each of us.

Where do we go, if we say "yes" to the Lord's call? The briefest description of the priestly mission—and this is true in its own way for men and women religious, too—has been given

25

to us by the Evangelist Mark. In his account of the call of the Twelve, he says, "Jesus appointed twelve to be with him and to be sent out" (Mk 3:14). To be with Jesus and, being sent, to go out to meet people—these two things belong together, and together they are the heart of a vocation, of the priesthood. To be with him and to be sent out—the two are inseparable. Only one who is "with him" comes to know him and can truly proclaim him. And anyone who has been with him cannot keep to himself what he has found; instead, he has to pass it on. Such was the case with Andrew, who told his brother Simon, "We have found the Messiah" (Jn 1:41). And the Evangelist adds, "He brought Simon to Jesus" (Jn 1:42). Pope Gregory the Great, in one of his homilies, once said that God's angels, however far afield they go on their missions, always move in God. They remain always with him. And while speaking about the angels, Saint Gregory thought also of bishops and priests: wherever they go, they should always "be with him." We know this from experience: whenever priests, because of their many duties, allot less and less time to being with the Lord, they eventually lose, for all their often heroic activity, the inner strength that sustains them. Their activity ends up as an empty activism. To be with Christ—how does this come about? Well, the first and most important thing for the priest is his daily Mass, always celebrated with deep interior participation. If we celebrate Mass truly as men of prayer, if we unite our words and our activities to the Word that precedes us and let them be shaped by the Eucharistic celebration, if in Communion we let ourselves truly be embraced by him and receive him—then we are being with him.

The Liturgy of the Hours is another fundamental way of being with Christ: here we pray as people conscious of our need to speak with God while lifting up all those others who have neither the time nor the ability to pray in this way. If our Eucharistic celebration and the Liturgy of the Hours are to remain meaningful, we need to devote ourselves constantly anew to the spiritual reading of sacred Scripture; not only to be able to decipher and explain words from the distant past, but to discover the word of comfort that the Lord is now speaking to me, the Lord who challenges me by this word. Only in this way will we be capable of bringing the inspired Word to the men and women of our time as the contemporary and living Word of God.

Eucharistic adoration is an essential way of being with the Lord. Thanks to Bishop Schraml, Altötting now has a new "treasury." Where once the treasures of the past were kept, precious historical and religious items, there is now a place for the Church's true treasure: the permanent presence of the Lord in his Sacrament. In one of his parables the Lord speaks of a treasure hidden in the field; whoever finds it sells all he has in order to buy that field, because the hidden treasure is more valuable than anything else. The hidden treasure, the good greater than any other good, is the Kingdom of God—it is Jesus himself, the Kingdom in person. In the sacred Host, he is present, the true treasure, always waiting for us. Only by adoring this presence do we learn how to receive him properly—we learn the reality of communion, we learn the Eucharistic celebration from the inside. Here I would like to quote some fine words of Saint Edith Stein, Co-Patroness of Europe, who wrote in one of her letters, "The Lord is present in the tabernacle in his divinity and his humanity. He is not there for himself, but for us: for it is his joy to be with us. He knows that we, being as we are, need to have him personally near. As a result, anyone with normal thoughts and feelings will naturally be drawn to spend time with him, whenever possible and as much as possible."[8] Let us love being with the Lord! There we can speak with him about everything. We can offer him our petitions, our concerns, our troubles. Our joys. Our gratitude, our disappointments, our needs, and our aspirations. There we can also constantly ask him, "Lord, send laborers into your harvest! Help me to be a good worker in your vineyard!"

Here in this Basilica, our thoughts turn to Mary, who lived her life fully "with Jesus" and consequently was, and continues to be, close to all men and women. The many votive plaques are a concrete sign of this. Let us think of Mary's holy mother, Saint Anne, and with her let us also think of the importance of mothers and fathers, of grandmothers and grandfathers, and the importance of the family as an environment of life and prayer, where we learn to pray and where vocations are able to develop.

Here in Altötting, we naturally think in a special way of good Brother Conrad. He renounced a great inheritance because he wanted to follow Jesus Christ unreservedly and to be completely with him. As the Lord recommended in the parable, he chose to take the lowest place, that of a humble lay—brother and porter. In his porter's lodge he was able to achieve exactly what Saint Mark tells us about the Apostles: "to stay with him," "to be sent" to others. From his cell he could always look at the

---

8. Edith Stein, "Philosophy of Psychology and the Humanities," in *The Collected Works of Edith Stein*, trans. Mary Catharine Baseheart and Marianne Sawicki (Washington, D.C.: ICS, 2000), 7:136ff.

THE MYSTERY OF VOCATION

tabernacle and thus always "stay with Christ." From this contemplation he learned the boundless goodness with which he
treated the people who would knock at his door at all hours—
sometimes mischievously, in order to provoke him, at other
times loudly and impatiently. To all of them, by his sheer goodness and humanity, and without grand words, he gave a message more valuable than words alone. Let us pray to Brother
Saint Conrad; let us ask him to help us to keep our gaze fixed on
the Lord, in order to bring God's love to the men and women of
our time. Amen!

4. Called to Holiness

From *Address of His Holiness Benedict XVI, Meeting with Young
People and Seminarians,* Apostolic Journey to the United States
of America and Visit to the United Nations Organization
Headquarters, Saint Joseph Seminary, Yonkers, New York,
April 19, 2008

"Proclaim the Lord Christ ... and always have your answer
ready for people who ask the reason for the hope that is within
you" (1 Pt 3:15). With these words from the First Letter of Peter I
greet each of you with heartfelt affection.

Young friends, I am very happy to have the opportunity to
speak with you. This evening I wish to share with you some
thoughts about being disciples of Jesus Christ—walking in the
Lord's footsteps, our own lives become a journey of hope.

In front of you are the images of six ordinary men and wom-
en who grew up to lead extraordinary lives. The Church hon-
ors them as Venerable, Blessed, or Saint: each responded to the

Lord's call to a life of charity and each served him here, in the alleys, streets, and suburbs of New York. I am struck by what a remarkably diverse group they are: poor and rich, lay men and women—one a wealthy wife and mother—priests and sisters, immigrants from afar, the daughter of a Mohawk warrior father and Algonquin mother, another a Haitian slave, and a Cuban intellectual.

Saint Elizabeth Ann Seton, Saint Frances Xavier Cabrini, Saint John Neumann, Blessed Kateri Tekakwitha, Venerable Pierre Toussaint, and Padre Felix Varela: any one of us could be among them, for there is no stereotype to this group, no single mold. Yet a closer look reveals that there are common elements. Inflamed with the love of Jesus, their lives became remarkable journeys of hope. For some, that meant leaving home and embarking on a pilgrim journey of thousands of miles. For each there was an act of abandonment to God, in the confidence that he is the final destination of every pilgrim. And all offered an outstretched hand of hope to those they encountered along the way, often awakening in them a life of faith. Through orphanages, schools, and hospitals, by befriending the poor, the sick, and the marginalized, and through the compelling witness that comes from walking humbly in the footsteps of Jesus, these six people laid open the way of faith, hope, and charity to countless individuals, including perhaps your own ancestors.

And what of today? Who bears witness to the Good News of Jesus on the streets of New York, in the troubled neighborhoods of large cities, in the places where the young gather, seeking someone in whom they can trust? God is our origin and our destination, and Jesus the way. The path of that journey twists and turns—just as it did for our saints—through the joys and the trials of ordinary, everyday life: within your families, at school or college, during your recreation activities, and in your parish communities. All these places are marked by the culture in which you are growing up. As young Americans you are offered many opportunities for personal development, and you are brought up with a sense of generosity, service, and fairness. Yet you do not need me to tell you that there are also difficulties: activities and mindsets that stifle hope, pathways that seem to lead to happiness and fulfillment but in fact end only in confusion and fear.

My own years as a teenager were marred by a sinister regime that thought it had all the answers; its influence grew—infiltrating schools and civic bodies, as well as politics and even religion—before it was fully recognized for the monster it was. It banished God and thus became impervious to anything true and good. Many of your grandparents and great-grandparents will have recounted the horror of the destruction that ensued. Indeed, some of them came to America precisely to escape such terror.

Let us thank God that today many people of your generation are able to enjoy the liberties that have arisen through the extension of democracy and respect for human rights. Let us thank God for all those who strive to ensure that you can grow up in an environment that nurtures what is beautiful, good, and true: your parents and grandparents, your teachers and priests, those civic leaders who seek what is right and just.

The power to destroy does, however, remain. To pretend otherwise would be to fool ourselves. Yet, it never triumphs; it is defeated. This is the essence of the hope that defines us as Christians; and the Church recalls this most dramatically during the Easter Triduum and celebrates it with great joy in the season of Easter! The One who shows us the way beyond death is the One who shows us how to overcome destruction and fear: thus it is Jesus who is the true teacher of life.[9] His death and resurrection mean that we can say to the Father "you have restored us to life!"[10] And so, just a few weeks ago, during the beautiful Easter Vigil liturgy, it was not from despair or fear that we cried out to God for our world, but with hope-filled confidence: dispel the darkness of our heart! Dispel the darkness of our minds![11]

What might that darkness be? What happens when people, especially the most vulnerable, encounter a clenched fist of repression or manipulation rather than a hand of hope? A first group of examples pertains to the heart. Here, the dreams and longings that young people pursue can so easily be shattered or destroyed. I am thinking of those affected by drug and substance abuse, homelessness and poverty, racism, violence, and degradation—especially of girls and women. While the causes of these problems are complex, all have in common a poisoned attitude of mind that results in people being treated as mere objects—a callousness of heart takes hold that first ignores, then ridicules, the God-given dignity of every human being. Such tragedies also point to what might have been and what could

9. Cf. Pope Benedict XVI, Encyclical Letter *Spe Salvi* (November 30, 2007), no. 6.

10. "Prayer After Communion, Good Friday," in *The Roman Missal*, trans. The International Commission on English in the Liturgy, 3rd typical ed., sec. 30 (Washington, D.C.: United States Catholic Conference of Bishops, 2011), 338.

11. Cf. "Prayer for the Blessing of the Fire and Preparation of the Candle," in *The Roman Missal*, sec. 14, 346.

be, were there other hands—your hands—reaching out. I encourage you to invite others, especially the vulnerable and the
innocent, to join you along the way of goodness and hope.

The second area of darkness—that which affects the mind—
often goes unnoticed, and for this reason is particularly sinister. The manipulation of truth distorts our perception of reality
and tarnishes our imagination and aspirations. I have already
mentioned the many liberties that you are fortunate enough to
enjoy. The fundamental importance of freedom must be rigor-
ously safeguarded. It is no surprise then that numerous individuals and groups vociferously claim their freedom in the public
forum. Yet freedom is a delicate value. It can be misunderstood
or misused so as to lead not to the happiness that we all expect
it to yield, but to a dark arena of manipulation in which our understanding of self and the world becomes confused or even distorted by those who have an ulterior agenda.

Have you noticed how often the call for freedom is made without ever referring to the truth of the human person? Some today
argue that respect for freedom of the individual makes it wrong
to seek truth, including the truth about what is good. In some cir-
cles to speak of truth is seen as controversial or divisive, and consequently best kept in the private sphere. And in truth's place—or
better said its absence—an idea has spread that, in giving value
to everything indiscriminately, claims to assure freedom and to
liberate conscience. This we call relativism. But what purpose has
a "freedom" that, in disregarding truth, pursues what is false or
wrong? How many young people have been offered a hand that
in the name of freedom or experience has led them to addiction,
to moral or intellectual confusion, to hurt, to a loss of self-respect,

even to despair and so tragically and sadly to the taking of their own life? Dear friends, truth is not an imposition. Nor is it simply a set of rules. It is a discovery of the One who never fails us; the One whom we can always trust. In seeking truth we come to live by belief because ultimately truth is a person: Jesus Christ. That is why authentic freedom is not an opting out. It is an opting in; nothing less than letting go of self and allowing oneself to be drawn into Christ's very being for others.[12]

How then can we as believers help others to walk the path of freedom that brings fulfillment and lasting happiness? Let us again turn to the saints. How did their witness truly free others from the darkness of heart and mind? The answer is found in the kernel of their faith; the kernel of our faith. The Incarnation, the birth of Jesus, tells us that God does indeed find a place among us. Though the inn is full, he enters through the stable, and there are people who see his light. They recognize Herod's dark closed world for what it is, and instead follow the bright guiding star of the night sky. And what shines forth? Here you might recall the prayer uttered on the most holy night of Easter: "Father we share in the light of your glory through your Son the light of the world ... inflame us with your hope!"[13] And so, in solemn procession with our lighted candles we pass the light of Christ among us. It is "the light which dispels all evil, washes guilt away, restores lost innocence, brings mourners joy, casts out hatred, brings us peace, and humbles earthly pride."[14]

---

12. Cf. Pope Benedict XVI, Encyclical Letter *Spe Salvi*, no. 28.

13. Cf. "Prayer for the Blessing of the Fire and Preparation of the Candle," in *The Roman Missal*, sec. 9–13, 348–53.

14. "The Easter Proclamation," in *The Roman Missal*, sec. 19, 348–53.

This is Christ's light at work. This is the way of the saints. It is a magnificent vision of hope—Christ's light beckons you to be guiding stars for others, walking Christ's way of forgiveness, reconciliation, humility, joy, and peace.

At times, however, we are tempted to close in on ourselves, to doubt the strength of Christ's radiance, to limit the horizon of hope. Take courage! Fix your gaze on our saints. The diversity of their experience of God's presence prompts us to discover anew the breadth and depth of Christianity. Let your imaginations soar freely along the limitless expanse of the horizons of Christian discipleship. Sometimes we are looked upon as people who speak only of prohibitions. Nothing could be further from the truth! Authentic Christian discipleship is marked by a sense of wonder. We stand before the God we know and love as a friend, the vastness of his creation, and the beauty of our Christian faith.

Dear friends, the example of the saints invites us, then, to consider four essential aspects of the treasure of our faith: personal prayer and silence, liturgical prayer, charity in action, and vocations.

What matters most is that you develop your personal relationship with God. That relationship is expressed in prayer. God by his very nature speaks, hears, and replies. Indeed, Saint Paul reminds us: we can and should "pray constantly" (1 Thes 5:17). Far from turning in on ourselves or withdrawing from the ups and downs of life, by praying we turn toward God and through him to each other, including the marginalized and those following ways other than God's path.[15] As the saints teach us so viv-

---

15. Cf. Pope Benedict XVI, Encyclical Letter *Spe Salvi*, no. 33.

idly, prayer becomes hope in action. Christ was their constant companion, with whom they conversed at every step of their journey for others.

There is another aspect of prayer that we need to remember: silent contemplation. Saint John, for example, tells us that to embrace God's revelation we must first listen, then respond by proclaiming what we have heard and seen.[16] Have we perhaps lost something of the art of listening? Do you leave space to hear God's whisper, calling you forth into goodness? Friends, do not be afraid of silence or stillness, listen to God, adore him in the Eucharist. Let his word shape your journey as an unfolding of holiness.

In the liturgy we find the whole Church at prayer. The word "liturgy" means the participation of God's people in "the work of Christ the Priest and of His Body which is the Church."[17] What is that work? First of all it refers to Christ's Passion, his Death and Resurrection, and his Ascension—what we call the Paschal Mystery. It also refers to the celebration of the liturgy itself. The two meanings are in fact inseparably linked because this "work of Jesus" is the real content of the liturgy. Through the liturgy, the "work of Jesus" is continually brought into contact with history; with our lives in order to shape them. Here we catch another glimpse of the grandeur of our Christian faith. Whenever you gather for Mass, when you go to Confession, whenever you celebrate any of the sacraments, Jesus is at work.

16. Cf. 1 Jn 1:2–3; Second Vatican Council, Dogmatic Constitution *Dei Verbum* (November 18, 1965), no. 1.

17. Second Vatican Council, Dogmatic Constitution *Sacrosanctum Concilium* (December 4, 1963), no. 7.

Through the Holy Spirit, he draws you to himself, into his sacrificial love of the Father which becomes love for all. We see then that the Church's liturgy is a ministry of hope for humanity. Your faithful participation is an active hope that helps to keep the world—saints and sinners alike—open to God; this is the truly human hope we offer everyone.[18]

Your personal prayer, your times of silent contemplation, and your participation in the Church's liturgy bring you closer to God and also prepare you to serve others. The saints accompanying us this evening show us that the life of faith and hope is also a life of charity. Contemplating Jesus on the Cross we see love in its most radical form. We can begin to imagine the path of love along which we must move.[19] The opportunities to make this journey are abundant. Look about you with Christ's eyes, listen with his ears, feel and think with his heart and mind. Are you ready to give all as he did for truth and justice? Many of the examples of the suffering which our saints responded to with compassion are still found here in this city and beyond. And new injustices have arisen: some are complex and stem from the exploitation of the heart and manipulation of the mind; even our common habitat, the earth itself, groans under the weight of consumerist greed and irresponsible exploitation. We must listen deeply. We must respond with a renewed social action that stems from the universal love that knows no bounds. In this way, we ensure that our works of mercy and justice become hope in action for others.

Dear young people, finally I wish to share a word about

18. Cf. Pope Benedict XVI, Encyclical Letter *Spe Salvi*, no. 34.
19. Pope Benedict XVI, Encyclical Letter *Deus Caritas Est* (December 25, 2005), no. 12.

vocations. First of all my thoughts go to your parents, grandparents, and godparents. They have been your primary educators in the faith. By presenting you for baptism, they made it possible for you to receive the greatest gift of your life. On that day you entered into the holiness of God himself. You became adoptive sons and daughters of the Father. You were incorporated into Christ. You were made a dwelling place of his Spirit. Let us pray for mothers and fathers throughout the world, particularly those who may be struggling in any way—socially, materially, spiritually. Let us honor the vocation of matrimony and the dignity of family life. Let us always appreciate that it is in families that vocations are given life.

Gathered here at Saint Joseph Seminary, I greet the seminarians present and indeed encourage all seminarians throughout America. I am glad to know that your numbers are increasing! The People of God look to you to be holy priests, on a daily journey of conversion, inspiring in others the desire to enter more deeply into the ecclesial life of believers. I urge you to deepen your friendship with Jesus the Good Shepherd. Talk heart to heart with him. Reject any temptation to ostentation, careerism, or conceit. Strive for a pattern of life truly marked by charity, chastity, and humility, in imitation of Christ, the Eternal High Priest, of whom you are to become living icons.[20] Dear seminarians, I pray for you daily. Remember that what counts before the Lord is to dwell in his love and to make his love shine forth for others.

Religious Sisters, Brothers, and Priests contribute greatly to

---

20. Cf. Pope John Paul II, Apostolic Exhortation *Pastores Dabo Vobis*, no. 33.

the mission of the Church. Their prophetic witness is marked by a profound conviction of the primacy with which the Gospel shapes Christian life and transforms society. Today, I wish to draw your attention to the positive spiritual renewal that Congregations are undertaking in relation to their charism. The word "charism" means a gift freely and graciously given. Charisms are bestowed by the Holy Spirit, who inspires founders and foundresses and shapes Congregations with a subsequent spiritual heritage. The wondrous array of charisms proper to each Religious Institute is an extraordinary spiritual treasury. Indeed, the history of the Church is perhaps most beautifully portrayed through the history of her schools of spirituality, most of which stem from the saintly lives of founders and foundresses. Through the discovery of charisms, which yield such a breadth of spiritual wisdom, I am sure that some of you young people will be drawn to a life of apostolic or contemplative service. Do not be shy to speak with Religious Brothers, Sisters, or Priests about the charism and spirituality of their Congregation. No perfect community exists, but it is fidelity to a founding charism, not to particular individuals, that the Lord calls you to discern. Have courage! You too can make your life a gift of self for the love of the Lord Jesus and, in him, of every member of the human family.[21]

Friends, again I ask you, what about today? What are you seeking? What is God whispering to you? The hope that never disappoints is Jesus Christ. The saints show us the selfless love of his way. As disciples of Christ, their extraordinary journeys

21. Cf. Pope John Paul II, Apostolic Exhortation *Vita Consecrata*, no. 3.

unfolded within the community of hope, which is the Church. It is from within the Church that you too will find the courage and support to walk the way of the Lord. Nourished by personal prayer, prompted in silence, shaped by the Church's liturgy, you will discover the particular vocation God has for you. Embrace it with joy. You are Christ's disciples today. Shine his light upon this great city and beyond. Show the world the reason for the hope that resonates within you. Tell others about the truth that sets you free.

5. Called to Be Missionaries

From *Message of His Holiness Pope Benedict XVI for the 45th World Day of Prayer for Vocations*, April 13, 2008

For the World Day of Prayer for Vocations, to be celebrated on April 13, 2008, I have chosen the theme *Vocations at the service of the Church on mission*. The Risen Jesus gave to the Apostles this command: "Go therefore and make disciples of all nations, baptizing them in the name of the Father and of the Son and of the Holy Spirit" (Mt 28:19), assuring them, "I am with you always, to the close of the age" (Mt 28:20). The Church is missionary in herself and in each one of her members. Through the sacraments of Baptism and Confirmation, every Christian is called to bear witness and to announce the Gospel, but this missionary dimension is associated in a special and intimate way with the priestly vocation. In the covenant with Israel, God entrusted to certain men, called by him and sent to the people in his name, a mission as prophets and priests. He did so, for example, with

Moses: "Come,—God told him—I will send you to Pharaoh, that you may bring forth my people ... out of Egypt ... when you have brought forth the people out of Egypt, you will serve God upon this mountain" (Ex 3:10, 12). The same happened with the prophets.

The promises made to our fathers were fulfilled entirely in Jesus Christ. In this regard, the Second Vatican Council says, "The Son, therefore, came, sent by the Father. It was in him, before the foundation of the world, that the Father chose us and predestined us to become adopted sons.... To carry out the will of the Father, Christ inaugurated the kingdom of heaven on earth and revealed to us the mystery of that kingdom. By his obedience he brought about redemption."[22] And Jesus already in his public life, while preaching in Galilee, chose some disciples to be his close collaborators in the messianic ministry. For example, on the occasion of the multiplication of the loaves, he said to the Apostles, "You give them something to eat" (Mt 14:16), encouraging them to assume the needs of the crowds to whom he wished to offer nourishment, but also to reveal the food "which endures to eternal life" (Jn 6:27). He was moved to compassion for the people, because while visiting cities and villages, he found the crowds weary and helpless, like sheep without a shepherd (cf. Mt 9:36). From this gaze of love came the invitation to his disciples: "Pray therefore the Lord of the harvest to send out laborers into his harvest" (Mt 9:38), and he sent the Twelve initially "to the lost sheep of the house of Israel" with precise instructions. If we pause to meditate on this

---

22. Cf. Second Vatican Council, Dogmatic Constitution *Lumen Gentium*, no. 3.

passage of Matthew's Gospel, commonly called the "missionary discourse," we may take note of those aspects that distinguish the missionary activity of a Christian community, eager to remain faithful to the example and teaching of Jesus. To respond to the Lord's call means facing in prudence and simplicity every danger and even persecutions, since "a disciple is not above his teacher, nor a servant above his master" (Mt 10:24). Having become one with their Master, the disciples are no longer alone as they announce the Kingdom of heaven; Jesus himself is acting in them: "He who receives you receives me, and he who receives me receives him who sent me" (Mt 10:40). Furthermore, as true witnesses, "clothed with power from on high" (Lk 24:49), they preach "repentance and the forgiveness of sins" (Lk 24:47) to all peoples.

Precisely because they have been sent by the Lord, the Twelve are called "Apostles," destined to walk the roads of the world announcing the Gospel as witnesses to the death and resurrection of Christ. Saint Paul, writing to the Christians of Corinth, says, "We—the Apostles—preach Christ crucified" (1 Cor 1:23). The Book of the Acts of the Apostles also assigns a very important role in this task of evangelization to other disciples whose missionary vocation arises from providential, sometimes painful, circumstances such as expulsion from their own lands for being followers of Jesus (cf. Acts 8:1–4). The Holy Spirit transforms this trial into an occasion of grace, using it so that the name of the Lord can be preached to other peoples, stretching in this way the horizons of the Christian community. These are men and women who, as Luke writes in the Acts of the Apostles, "have risked their lives for the sake of our Lord

Jesus Christ" (Acts 15:26). First among them is undoubtedly Paul of Tarsus, called by the Lord himself, hence a true Apostle. The story of Paul, the greatest missionary of all times, brings out in many ways the link between vocation and mission. Accused by his opponents of not being authorized for the apostolate, he makes repeated appeals precisely to the call that he received directly from the Lord (cf. Rom 1:1; Gal 1:11–12, 15–17).

In the beginning, and thereafter, what "impels" the Apostles (cf. 2 Cor 5:14) is always "the love of Christ." Innumerable missionaries, throughout the centuries, as faithful servants of the Church, docile to the action of the Holy Spirit, have followed in the footsteps of the first disciples. The Second Vatican Council notes, "Although every disciple of Christ, as far in him lies, has the duty of spreading the faith, Christ the Lord always calls whomever he will from among the number of his disciples, to be with him and to be sent by him to preach to the nations."[23] In fact, the love of Christ must be communicated to the brothers by example and words, with all one's life. My venerable predecessor John Paul II wrote, "The special vocation of missionaries 'for life' retains all its validity: it is the model of the Church's missionary commitment, which always stands in need of radical and total self-giving, of new and bold endeavors."[24]

Among those totally dedicated to the service of the Gospel are priests, called to preach the word of God, administer the sacraments, especially the Eucharist and Reconciliation, committed

---

23. Cf. Mk 3:13–15; Second Vatican Council, Decree *Ad Gentes* (December 7, 1965), no. 23.

24. Pope John Paul II, Encyclical Letter *Redemptoris Missio* (December 7, 1990), no. 66.

to helping the lowly, the sick, the suffering, the poor, and those who experience hardship in areas of the world where there are, at times, many who still have not had a real encounter with Jesus Christ. Missionaries announce for the first time to these people Christ's redemptive love. Statistics show that the number of baptized persons increases every year, thanks to the pastoral work of these priests, who are wholly consecrated to the salvation of their brothers and sisters. In this context, a special word of thanks must be expressed "to the *fidei donum* priests who work faithfully and generously at building up the community by proclaiming the word of God and breaking the Bread of Life, devoting all their energy to serving the mission of the Church. Let us thank God for all the priests who have suffered even to the sacrifice of their lives in order to serve Christ.... Theirs is a moving witness that can inspire many young people to follow Christ and to expend their lives for others, and thus to discover true life."[25]

There have always been in the Church many men and women who, prompted by the action of the Holy Spirit, choose to live the Gospel in a radical way, professing the vows of chastity, poverty, and obedience. This multitude of men and women religious, belonging to innumerable Institutes of contemplative and active life, still plays "the main role in the evangelization of the world."[26] With their continual and community prayer, contemplatives intercede without ceasing for all humanity. Religious of the active life, with their many charitable activities, bring to all a living witness of the love and mercy of God. The Servant of God

25. Cf. Pope Benedict XVI, Apostolic Exhortation *Sacramentum Caritatis* (February 22, 2007), no. 26.
26. Second Vatican Council, Decree *Ad Gentes*, no. 40.

Paul VI concerning these apostles of our times said, "Thanks to their consecration they are eminently willing and free to leave everything and to go and proclaim the Gospel even to the ends of the earth. They are enterprising and their apostolate is often marked by an originality, by a genius that demands admiration. They are generous: often they are found at the outposts of the mission, and they take the greatest of risks for their health and their very lives. Truly the Church owes them much."[27]

Furthermore, so that the Church may continue to fulfill the mission entrusted to her by Christ, and not lack promoters of the Gospel so badly needed by the world, Christian communities must never fail to provide both children and adults with constant education in the faith. It is necessary to keep alive in the faithful a committed sense of missionary responsibility and active solidarity with the peoples of the world. The gift of faith calls all Christians to cooperate in the work of evangelization. This awareness must be nourished by preaching and catechesis, by the liturgy, and by constant formation in prayer. It must grow through the practice of welcoming others, with charity and spiritual companionship, through reflection and discernment, as well as pastoral planning, of which attention to vocations must be an integral part.

Vocations to the ministerial priesthood and to the consecrated life can only flourish in a spiritual soil that is well cultivated. Christian communities that live the missionary dimension of the mystery of the Church in a profound way will never be inward looking. Mission, as a witness of divine love, becomes

27. Pope Paul VI, Apostolic Exhortation *Evangelii Nuntiandi* (December 8, 1975), no. 69.

particularly effective when it is shared in a community, "so that the world may believe" (cf. Jn 17:21). The Church prays every day to the Holy Spirit for the gift of vocations. Gathered around the Virgin Mary, Queen of the Apostles, as in the beginning, the ecclesial community learns from her how to implore the Lord for a flowering of new apostles, alive with the faith and love that are necessary for the mission.

While I entrust this reflection to all the ecclesial communities so that they may make it their own, and draw from it inspiration for prayer, and as I encourage those who are committed to work with faith and generosity in the service of vocations, I wholeheartedly send to educators, catechists, and to all, particularly to young people on their vocational journey, a special Apostolic Blessing.

6. *A Human Response to a Divine Initiative*

From *Message of His Holiness Pope Benedict XVI for the 46th World Day of Prayer for Vocations*, May 3, 2009

On the occasion of the next World Day of Prayer for vocations to the priesthood and to the consecrated life, which will be celebrated on May 3, 2009, the Fourth Sunday of Easter, I want to invite all the People of God to reflect on the theme *Faith in the divine initiative—the human response*. The exhortation of Jesus to his disciples, "Pray therefore the Lord of the harvest to send out laborers into his harvest" (Mt 9:38), has a constant resonance in the Church. Pray! The urgent call of the Lord stresses that prayer for vocations should be continuous and trusting. The

Christian community can only really "have ever greater faith and hope in God's providence" if it is enlivened by prayer.[28]

The vocation to the priesthood and to the consecrated life constitutes a special gift of God that becomes part of the great plan of love and salvation that God has for every man and woman and for the whole of humanity. The Apostle Paul, whom we remember in a special way during this Pauline Year dedicated to the two-thousandth anniversary of his birth, writing to the Ephesians, says, "Blessed be the God and Father of our Lord Jesus Christ, who has blessed us in Christ with every spiritual blessing in the heavenly places, even as he chose us in him before the foundation of the world, that we should be holy and blameless before him" (Eph 1:3–4). In the universal call to holiness, of particular relevance is God's initiative of choosing some to follow his Son Jesus Christ more closely, and to be his privileged ministers and witnesses. The divine Master personally called the Apostles "to be with him, and to be sent out to preach and have authority to cast out demons" (Mk 3:14–15); they, in turn, gathered other disciples around them as faithful collaborators in this mission. In this way, responding to the Lord's call and docile to the movement of the Holy Spirit, over the centuries, countless ranks of priests and consecrated persons placed themselves totally at the service of the Gospel in the Church. Let us give thanks to God, because even today he continues to call together workers into his vineyard. While it is undoubtedly true that a worrisome shortage of priests is evident in some regions of the world, and that the Church encounters difficulties

28. Pope Benedict XVI, Apostolic Exhortation *Sacramentum Caritatis*, no. 26.

and obstacles along the way, we are sustained by the unshakable certitude that the one who firmly guides her in the pathways of time toward the definitive fulfillment of the Kingdom is he, the Lord, who freely chooses persons of every culture and of every age and invites them to follow him according to the mysterious plans of his merciful love.

Our first duty, therefore, is to keep alive in families and in parishes, in movements and in apostolic associations, in religious communities and in all the sectors of diocesan life this appeal to the divine initiative with unceasing prayer. We must pray that the whole Christian people grows in its trust in God, convinced that the "Lord of the harvest" does not cease to ask some to place their entire existence freely at his service so as to work with him more closely in the mission of salvation. What is asked of those who are called, for their part, is careful listening and prudent discernment, a generous and willing adherence to the divine plan, and a serious study of the reality that is proper to the priestly and religious vocations, so as to be able to respond responsibly and with conviction.

The *Catechism of the Catholic Church* rightly reminds us that God's free initiative requires a free response on the part of men and women; a positive response that always presupposes acceptance of and identification with the plan that God has for everyone; a response that welcomes the Lord's loving initiative and becomes, for the one who is called, a binding moral imperative, an offering of thanksgiving to God, and a total cooperation with the plan that God carries out in history.[29]

---

29. *Catechism of the Catholic Church* (1993), no. 2062.

Contemplating the mystery of the Eucharist, which expresses in a sublime way the free gift of the Father in the Person of
his Only Begotten Son for the salvation of mankind, and the full
and docile readiness of Christ to drink to the dregs the "cup" of
the will of God (cf. Mt 26:39), we can more readily understand
how "*faith in the divine initiative*" models and gives value to the
"*human response.*" In the Eucharist, that perfect gift that brings
to fulfillment the plan of love for the redemption of the world,
Jesus offers himself freely for the salvation of mankind. "The
Church," my beloved predecessor John Paul II wrote, "has received the Eucharist from Christ her Lord not as a gift—however precious—among so many others, but as the *gift par excellence*,
for it is the gift of himself, of his person in his sacred humanity,
as well as the gift of his saving work."[30]

It is priests who are called to perpetuate this salvific mystery from century to century until the Lord's glorious return,
for they can contemplate, precisely in the Eucharistic Christ,
the eminent model of a "vocational dialogue" between the free
initiative of the Father and the faithful response of Christ. In
the celebration of the Eucharist it is Christ himself who acts in
those whom he chooses as his ministers; he supports them so
that their response develops in a dimension of trust and gratitude that removes all fear, even when they experience more
acutely their own weakness (cf. Rom 8:26–28), or indeed when
the experience of misunderstanding or even of persecution is
most bitter (cf. Rom 8:35–39).

The awareness of being saved by the love of Christ, which

---

30. Pope John Paul II, Encyclical Letter *Ecclesia de Eucharistia* (April 17, 2003), no. 11.

every Mass nourishes in the faithful and especially in priests, cannot but arouse within them a trusting self-abandonment to Christ who gave his life for us. To believe in the Lord and to accept his gift, therefore, leads us to entrust ourselves to Him with thankful hearts, adhering to his plan of salvation. When this does happen, the one who is "called" voluntarily leaves everything and submits himself to the teaching of the divine Master; hence a fruitful dialogue between God and man begins, a mysterious encounter between the love of the Lord who calls and the freedom of man who responds in love, hearing the words of Jesus echoing in his soul, "You did not choose me, but I chose you and appointed you that you should go and bear fruit and that your fruit should abide" (Jn 15:16).

This intertwining of love between the divine initiative and the human response is present also, in a wonderful way, in the vocation to the consecrated life. The Second Vatican Council recalls, "The evangelical counsels of chastity dedicated to God, poverty, and obedience are based upon the words and examples of the Lord. They were further commanded by the apostles and Fathers of the Church, as well as by the doctors and pastors of souls. The counsels are a divine gift, which the Church received from its Lord and which it always safeguards with the help of His grace."[31]

Once more, Jesus is the model of complete and trusting adherence to the will of the Father, to whom every consecrated person must look. Attracted by him, from the very first centuries of Christianity, many men and women have left families, posses-

---

31. Second Vatican Council, Pastoral Constitution *Lumen Gentium*, no. 43.

sions, material riches, and all that is humanly desirable in order to follow Christ generously and live the Gospel without compromise, which had become for them a school of deeply rooted holiness. Today, too, many undertake this same demanding journey of evangelical perfection and realize their vocation in the profession of the evangelical counsels. The witness of these our brothers and sisters, in contemplative monasteries, religious institutes, and congregations of apostolic life, reminds the people of God "that mystery of the Kingdom of God is already at work in history, even as it awaits its full realization in heaven."[32]

Who can consider himself worthy to approach the priestly ministry? Who can embrace the consecrated life relying only on his or her own human powers? Once again, it is useful to reiterate that the response of men and women to the divine call, whenever they are aware that it is God who takes the initiative and brings His plan of salvation to fulfillment, is never patterned after the timid self-interest of the worthless servant who, out of fear, hid the talent entrusted to him in the ground (cf. Mt 25:14–30), but rather expresses itself in a ready adherence to the Lord's invitation, as in the case of Peter who, trusting in the Lord's word, did not hesitate to let down the net once more even after having toiled all night and catching nothing (cf. Lk 5:5). Without in any sense renouncing personal responsibility, the free human response to God thus becomes "co-responsibility," responsibility in and with Christ, through the action of his Holy Spirit; it becomes communion with the One who makes it possible for us to bear much fruit (cf. Jn 15:5).

---

32. Pope John Paul II, Apostolic Exhortation *Vita Consecrata*, no. 1.

An emblematic human response, full of trust in God's initiative, is the generous and unmitigated "Amen" of the Virgin of Nazareth, uttered with humble and decisive adherence to the plan of the Most High announced to her by God's messenger (cf. Lk 1:38). Her prompt "Yes" allowed her to become the Mother of God, the Mother of our Savior. Mary, after this first "fiat," had to repeat it many times, even up to the culminating moment of the crucifixion of Jesus, when "standing by the cross of Jesus," as the Evangelist John notes, she participated in the dreadful suffering of her innocent Son. And it was from the cross that Jesus, while dying, gave her to us as Mother and entrusted us to her as sons and daughters (cf. Jn 19:26–27); she is especially the Mother of priests and consecrated persons. I want to entrust to her all those who are aware of God's call to set out on the road of the ministerial priesthood or consecrated life.

Dear friends, do not become discouraged in the face of difficulties and doubts; trust in God and follow Jesus faithfully and you will be witnesses of the joy that flows from intimate union with him. Imitating the Virgin Mary whom all generations proclaim as blessed because she believed (cf. Lk 1:48), commit yourselves with every spiritual energy to realize the heavenly Father's plan of salvation, cultivating in your heart, like her, the ability to be astonished and to adore him who is mighty and does "great things," for Holy is his name (cf. Lk 1:49).

7. Called to Freedom

From *Address of His Holiness Benedict XVI to the Community of the
Roman Major Seminary for the Annual Feast of Our Lady of Trust,*
February 20, 2009

It is always a great joy for me to be in my Seminary, to see
the future priests of my Diocese, to be with you under the sign
of Our Lady of Trust. With the one who helps and accompanies
us, who gives us real certainty in being always assisted by divine grace, and we go forward!

Now we wish to see what St. Paul tells us with this text:
"You were called to freedom" (Gal 5:13). Since the beginning and
throughout all time but especially in the modern age freedom
has been the great dream of humanity. We know that Luther
was inspired by this passage from the Letter to the Galatians
and that he concluded that the monastic Rule, the hierarchy, the
Magisterium seemed to him as a yoke of slavery from which it
was necessary to liberate oneself. Subsequently, the Age of Enlightenment was totally guided, penetrated, by this desire for
freedom, which was considered to have finally been reached.
But Marxism too presented itself as a road toward freedom.

We ask ourselves this evening: what is freedom? How can
we be free? St. Paul helps us to understand this complicated
reality that is freedom, inserting this concept into fundamen-
tally anthropological and theological context. He says, "Do not
use your freedom as an opportunity for self-indulgence, but
through love be servants of one another" (Gal 5:13). The Rector
has already told us that the "flesh" is not the body, but, in the

language of St. Paul, "flesh" is an expression of the absolutization of self, of the self that wants to be all and to take all for its own. The absolute "I" who depends on nothing and on no one seems to possess freedom truly and definitively. I am free if I depend on no one, if I can do anything I want. But exactly this absolutization of the "I" is "flesh," which is a degradation of man. It is not the conquest of freedom: libertinism is not freedom, but rather freedom's failure.

And Paul dares to propose a strong paradox: "Through love, be servants" (Gal 5:13) (in Greek: *douléuete*). In other words, freedom, paradoxically, is achieved in service. We become free if we become servants of one another. And so Paul places the whole matter of freedom in the light of the truth of man. To reduce oneself to flesh, seemingly elevating oneself to divine status, "I alone am the man," leads to deception. Because in reality it is not so: man is not an absolute, as if the "I" can isolate itself and behave only according to its own will. It is contrary to the truth of our being. Our truth is that above all we are creatures, creatures of God, and we live in relationship with the Creator. We are relational beings. And only by accepting our relationality can we enter into the truth; otherwise we fall into deception, and in it, in the end, we destroy ourselves.

We are creatures, therefore dependent on the Creator. In the Age of Enlightenment, to atheism especially this appeared as a dependence from which it was necessary to free oneself. In reality, however, it would be only a fatal dependence were this God Creator a tyrant and not a good Being, were this God like any human tyrants. If, instead, this Creator loves us, and our dependence means being within the space of his love, in that case it is precisely dependence that is freedom. In this way we are in fact within the charity of the Creator; we are united to him, to the whole of his reality, to all of his power. Therefore, this is the first point: to be a creature means to be loved by the Creator, to be in this relationship of love that he gives us, through which he provides for us. From this derives first of all our truth, which is at the same time a call to charity.

Therefore, to see God, to orient oneself to God, know God, know God's will, enter into the will that is, into the love of God is to enter ever more into the space of truth. And this journey of coming to know God, of loving relationship with God, is the extraordinary adventure of our Christian life; for in Christ we know the face of God, the face of God that loves us even unto the Cross, unto the gift of himself.

But creaturely relationality implies a second type of relationship, as well. We are in relationship with God, but together, as a human family, we are also in relationship with each other. In other words, human freedom is, in part, being within the joy and ample space of God's love, but it also implies becoming one with the other and for the other. There is no freedom in opposing the other. If I make myself the absolute, I become the enemy of the other; we can no longer live together, and the whole of life becomes cruelty, becomes a failure. Only a shared freedom is a human freedom; in being together we can enter into the harmony of freedom.

And therefore this is another very important point: only in the acceptance of the other, accepting also the apparent limitations on my freedom that derive from respect for that of the other, only by entering into the net of dependence that finally makes us a single family am I on the path to communal freedom.

Here a very important element appears: what is the measure of sharing freedom? We see that man needs order, laws, so that he can realize his freedom that is a freedom lived in common. And how can we find this correct order, in which no one is oppressed but rather each one can give his contribution to form this sort of concert of freedoms? If there is no common truth of man as it appears in the vision of God, only positivism remains, and one has the impression of something imposed in an even violent manner. From this emerges rebellion against order and law as though it entails slavery.

But if we can find the order of the Creator in our nature, the order of truth that gives each one his place, then order and law can be the very instruments of freedom against the slavery of selfishness. To serve one another becomes the instrument of freedom, and here we could add a whole philosophy of politics according to the Social Doctrine of the Church, which helps us to find this common order that gives each one his place in the common life of humanity. The first reality meriting respect, therefore, is the truth: freedom opposed to truth is not freedom. To serve one another creates the common space of freedom.

And then Paul continues, saying, "The whole law is fulfilled in one word, namely, 'You shall love your neighbor as yourself'" (Gal 5:14). Behind this affirmation appears the mystery of God Incarnate, appears the mystery of Christ who in his life, in his death, in his Resurrection becomes the living law. The first words of our Reading, "You were called to freedom," alluded directly to this mystery. We have been called by the Gospel, we have truly been called in Baptism, in the participation in the death and Resurrection of Christ. In this way we have passed from the "flesh," from selfishness to communion with Christ. And thus we are in the fullness of the law.

You probably all know the beautiful words of St. Augustine: *"Dilige et fac quod vis,"* that is, "love and do what you will."[33] What Augustine says is the truth, if we have well understood the word "love." "Love and do what you will," but we must really be in communion with Christ, penetrated by him, identifying ourselves with his death and Resurrection and united to him in the communion of his Body. By participating in the sacraments, by listening to the word of God truly the divine will, the divine law, enters into our will. Our will identifies with his, we become one single will, and thus we can truly be freed; we can truly do what we want to do; because we want with Christ, we want in the truth and with the truth.

Therefore, let us pray the Lord to help us in this journey that began with Baptism, a journey of identification with Christ that is fulfilled ever anew in the Eucharist. In the Third Eucharistic Prayer we say "that we ... become one body, one spirit in Christ."[34] It is a moment in which, through the Eucharist and through our true participation in the mystery of Christ's death and Resurrection, we become one spirit with him. We exist in this identity of will, and thus we truly reach freedom.

Behind these words the law is fulfilled; behind this single statement that becomes reality in communion with Christ,

33. Augustine, *Opera Exegetica* 7.4.7, *Patrologia Cursus Completus,* Patrologia Latina, ed. Jacques P. Migne (Paris: 1844–64), 35:2033.

34. "Third Eucharistic Prayer," in *The Roman Missal,* sec. 113, 653.

there appear behind the Lord the figures of all the Saints who have entered into this communion with Christ. They appear in this unity of being, in this unity with his will. Our Lady appears foremost, in her humility, in her goodness, in her love. Our Lady gives us this trust, takes us by the hand, guides us, helps us along the path of becoming united to the will of God as she has been from her first moment, having expressed this union in her "*Fiat.*"

And finally, after these beautiful things, once again in the Letter there is mention of a slightly sad situation in the Galatians' community, when Paul says, "If you bite and devour one another take care that you are not consumed by one another.... Walk by the Spirit." It seems to me that in this community, which was no longer on the path of communion with Christ, but of the exterior law of the "flesh," polemics naturally surfaced also, and Paul says, "You have become wild beasts, one biting the other." Thus he alludes to the polemics that are born where faith degenerates into intellectualism and humility is substituted by the arrogance of being better than the other.

We see well that today too there are similar things where instead of entering into communion with Christ, in the Body of Christ that is the Church everyone wants to be better than everyone else, and with intellectual arrogance each wants to make it known that he or she is the best. And this leads to destructive polemics, born from a caricature of the Church that should be of one soul and one heart.

In this warning of St. Paul we must also today find a reason for an examination of conscience: not to think ourselves above others, but to bring ourselves into Christ's humility, into Our

Lady's humility, to enter into the obedience of faith. Precisely in this way does the great space of truth and freedom in love truly open before us, too.

Lastly, we want to thank God because he has shown us his face in Christ, because he has given us Our Lady, he has given us the Saints; he has called us to be one body, one spirit with him. And we pray that he may help us to be ever more engaged in this communion with his will, thus to find ourselves within his freedom, love, and joy.

8. Called to Serve

From *Address by the Holy Father*, Celebration
of Vespers with Priests, Men and Women Religious,
Seminarians, and Lay Movements, Prague,
September 26, 2009

I greet all of you in the words of Saint Paul that we have just heard in our Scripture reading: *Grace and peace to you from God our Father!* First of all I address these words to the Cardinal Archbishop, whom I thank for his gracious words. I extend my greeting to the other Cardinals and Bishops present, to the priests and deacons, the seminarians, men and women religious, to the catechists and pastoral workers, to the young people, the families, and to the representatives of ecclesial associations and movements.

We are gathered this evening in a place that is dear to you, a place that is a visible sign of the power of divine grace acting in the hearts of believers. The beauty of this thousand-year-old church is indeed a living testimony to your people's rich history of faith and Christian tradition: a history that is illuminated in particular by the faithfulness of those who sealed their adherence to Christ and to the Church by martyrdom. I am thinking of Saint Wenceslaus, Saint Adalbert, and Saint John Nepomuk, milestones in your Church's history, to whom we may add the example of the young Saint Vitus, who preferred to die a martyr's death rather than betray Christ, and the examples of the monk Saint Procopius and Saint Ludmila. From the twentieth century, I recall the experiences of two Archbishops of this local church, Cardinals Josef Beran and František Tomášek, and of many Bishops, priests, men and women religious, and lay faithful, who resisted Communist persecution with heroic fortitude, even to the sacrifice of their lives. Where did these courageous friends of Christ find their strength if not from the Gospel? Indeed, they were captivated by Jesus who said, "If any man would come after me, let him deny himself and take up his cross and follow me" (Mt 16:24). In the hour of trial they heard another saying of Jesus resounding deep within them: "If they persecuted me, they will persecute you" (Jn 15:20).

The heroism of these witnesses to the faith reminds us that only through personal intimacy and a profound bond with Christ is it possible to draw the spiritual vitality needed to live the Christian vocation to the full. Only the love of Christ can make the apostolate effective, especially in moments of difficulty and trial. Love for Christ and for one's fellow men and women must be the hallmark of every Christian and every community. In the Acts of the Apostles we read that "the company of those who believed were of one heart and soul" (Acts 4:32). Tertullian, an early Church writer, noted that pagans were impressed by the love that bound Christians together.[35] Dear brothers and sisters, imitate the divine Master who "came not to be served, but to serve and to give his life as a ransom for many" (Mk 10:45). Let love shine forth in each of your parishes and communities, and in your various associations and movements. According to the image used by Saint Paul, let your Church be a well-structured body with Christ as Head, in which every member acts in harmony with the whole. Nourish your love for Christ by prayer and by listening to his word; feed on him in the Eucharist, and by his grace, be builders of unity and peace wherever you go.

Twenty years ago, after the long winter of Communist dictatorship, your Christian communities began once more to express themselves freely, when, through the events triggered by the student demonstration of November 17, 1989, your people regained their freedom. Yet you are well aware that even today it is not easy to live and bear witness to the Gospel. Society continues to suffer from the wounds caused by atheist ideology, and it is often seduced by the modern mentality of hedonistic consumerism amid a dangerous crisis of human and religious values and a growing drift toward ethical and cultural relativism. In this context there is an urgent need for renewed effort throughout the Church so as to strengthen spiritual and moral values in present-day society. I know that your communities are already actively engaged on several fronts, especially in charitable work, carried out under the auspices of *Caritas*. Your pastoral activity in the field of educating new generations should be undertaken with particular zeal. Catholic schools should foster

---

35. Cf. Tertullian, *Apologeticum* 39.7.

respect for the human person; attention should also be given to the pastoral care of young people outside the school environment, without neglecting other groups of the faithful. Christ is for everyone! I sincerely hope that there will be a growing accord with other institutions, both public and private. It is always worth repeating that the Church does not seek privileges, but only to be able to work freely in the service of all, in the spirit of the Gospel.

Dear brothers and sisters, may the Lord in his goodness make you like the salt spoken of in the Gospel, salt that gives savor to life, so that you may be faithful laborers in the Lord's vineyard. Dear Bishops and priests, it is your task to work tirelessly for the good of those entrusted to your care. Always draw inspiration from the Gospel image of the Good Shepherd, who knows his sheep, calls them by name, leads them to safe pastures, and is prepared to give his life for them (cf. Jn 10:1–19). Dear consecrated persons, by professing the evangelical counsels you recall the primacy that each of us must give to God in our lives. By living in community, you bear witness to the enrichment that comes from practicing the commandment of love (cf. Jn 13:34). By your fidelity to this vocation, you will help the men and women of today to let themselves be captivated by God and by the Gospel of his Son.[36] And you, dear young people in seminaries or houses of formation, be sure to acquire a solid cultural, spiritual, and pastoral preparation. In this Year for Priests, with which I chose to mark the 150th anniversary of the death of the Curé d'Ars, may you learn from the example of this pastor who was completely dedicated to God and to the care of

36. Cf. Pope John Paul II, Apostolic Exhortation *Vita Consecrata*, no. 104.

souls; he was well aware that it was his ministry, nourished by prayer, that constituted his path to sanctification.

Dear Brothers and Sisters, with gratitude to the Lord, we shall be marking a number of anniversaries this year: the 280th anniversary of the canonization of Saint John Nepomuk, the eightieth anniversary of the dedication of Saint Vitus's Cathedral, and the twentieth anniversary of the canonization of Saint Agnes of Bohemia, the event that heralded your country's deliverance from atheist oppression. All these are good reasons for persevering in the journey of faith with joy and enthusiasm, counting on the maternal intercession of Mary, Mother of God, and all your Patron Saints.

9. The World Needs Witnesses

From *Address of His Holiness Benedict XVI*, Celebration of
Vespers with Priests, Religious, Seminarians and Deacons,
Fátima, Wednesday, May 12, 2010

"When the time had fully come, God sent forth his Son born of woman, ... so that we might receive adoption as sons" (Gal 4:4–5). The fullness of time came when the Eternal broke into time; by the grace of the Holy Spirit the Son of the Most High was conceived and became man in the womb of a woman, the Virgin Mary, type and lofty model of the believing Church. The Church does not cease to beget new sons in the Son, whom the Father willed to be the first-born of many brothers. Each one of us is called to be with Mary and like Mary, a humble and simple sign of the Church who offers herself constantly as a spouse into the hands of her Lord.

To all of you who have given your life to Christ I wish to express this evening the Church's appreciation and recognition. Thank you for your witness, often silent and certainly not easy; thank you for your fidelity to the Gospel and to the Church. In Jesus, present in the Eucharist, I embrace my brothers in the priesthood and the deacons, the consecrated women and men, the seminarians and the members of the movements and new ecclesial communities present. May the Lord reward, as he alone can and does, all those who have made it possible for us to gather together before the presence of Jesus in the Eucharist. I mention especially the Episcopal Commission for Vocations and Ministries, with its President, Bishop António Santos, whom I thank for his greeting, full of collegial and fraternal affection, at the beginning of Vespers. In this "upper room" of faith that is Fátima, the Virgin Mother shows us the way to place our pure and holy offering into the hands of the Father.

Let me open my heart and tell you that the greatest concern of every Christian, especially of every consecrated person or minister of the altar, must be fidelity, loyalty to one's own vocation, as a disciple who wishes to follow the Lord. Faithfulness over time is the name of love, of a consistent, true, and profound love for Christ the Priest. "Since Baptism is a true entry into the holiness of God through incorporation into Christ and the indwelling of his Spirit, it would be a contradiction to settle for a life of mediocrity, marked by a minimalistic ethic and a shallow religiosity."[37] In this Year for Priests that is drawing to its close, may grace in abundance come down upon you that you may live joyfully your

---

37. Pope John Paul II, Apostolic Letter *Novo Millennio Ineunte* (January 6, 2001), no. 31.

consecration and bear witness to your priestly fidelity grounded in the fidelity of Christ. This evidently supposes true intimacy with Christ in prayer, since it is the powerful and intense experience of the Lord's love that brings priests and consecrated persons to respond to his love in a way that is exclusive and spousal.

This life of special consecration was born to keep the Gospel always before the People of God as a reminder that manifests, certifies, and proclaims to the whole Church the radical nature of the Gospel and the coming of the Kingdom. Dear consecrated men and women, by your dedication to prayer, asceticism, and growth in the spiritual life, to apostolic action and mission, you are progressing toward the heavenly Jerusalem, you are a foretaste of the eschatological Church, solid in her possession and loving contemplation of God who is love. How much we need this witness today! Many of our brothers and sisters live as if there were nothing beyond this life, and without concern for their eternal salvation. Men and women are called to know and love God, and the Church has the mission to assist them in this calling. We know well that God is the master of his gifts and that conversion is a grace. But we are responsible for proclaiming the faith, the whole faith, with all its demands. Dear friends, let us imitate the Curé of Ars who prayed to the Lord in the following words: "Grant me the conversion of my parish, and I accept to suffer all that you wish for the rest of my life." And he did everything to pull people away from their own lukewarm attitude in order to lead them back to love.

There exists a deep solidarity among all the members of the Body of Christ. It is not possible to love Christ without loving his brothers and sisters. For their salvation John Mary Vianney decided to become a priest "to win souls for the good God,"[38] as he said when, at eighteen years of age, he announced his vocation, just as Paul had said: "to win as many as I could" (1 Cor 9:19). The Vicar General had told him, "there is not much love of God in the parish; you will bring it there." In his priestly passion, this holy parish priest was merciful like Jesus in meeting each sinner. He preferred to insist on the attractive aspect of virtue, on God's mercy, in comparison to which our sins are like "grains of sand." He pointed to the merciful love of God that had been offended. He feared that priests would become "insensitive" and accustomed to the indifference of their faithful: "Woe to the Pastor"—he would warn—"who remains silent while God is offended and souls are lost."[39]

Dear brother priests, in this place, which Mary has made special, keep before your eyes her vocation as a faithful disciple of her Son Jesus from the moment of his conception to the Cross, and then beyond, along the path of the nascent Church, and consider the unheard-of grace of your priesthood. Fidelity to one's vocation requires courage and trust, but the Lord also wishes that you join forces: that you be concerned for one another and support one another fraternally. Moments of common prayer and study, and sharing in the demands of the priestly life and work, are a necessary part of your life. It is a fine thing when you welcome one another into your homes with the peace of Christ in your hearts! It is important to assist one another with prayer, helpful advice, and discernment! Be especially attentive to those situations where there is a certain weakening of priestly

---

38. Alfred Monnin, *Life of the Curé d'Ars* (London: Burns and Lambert, 1862), 23.
39. Ibid.

ideals or dedication to activities not fully consonant with what is proper for a minister of Jesus Christ. Then is the time to take a firm stand, with an attitude of warm fraternal love, as brother assisting his brother to "remain on his feet."

The priesthood of Christ is eternal (cf. Heb 5:6), but the life of priests is limited. Christ has willed that others continue in time the priestly ministry that he instituted. Keep alive in your hearts, and in others around you, the desire to raise up—in cooperation with the grace of the Holy Spirit—new priestly vocations among the faithful. Trustful and persevering prayer, joyful love of one's own vocation, and commitment to the work of spiritual direction will allow you to discern the charism of vocation in those whom God calls.

Dear seminarians, who have taken the first step toward the priesthood and are preparing in the major seminary or in houses of formation, the Pope encourages you to be conscious of the great responsibility that you will have to assume. Carefully examine your intentions and your motivations. Devote yourselves with a steadfast heart and a generous spirit to your training. The Eucharist, which is the center of Christian life and the school of humility and service, should be your first love. Adoration, piety, and care for the Most Holy Sacrament during these years of preparation will lead you one day to celebrate the Sacrifice of the Altar in an edifying and devout manner.

Along this path of fidelity, beloved priests and deacons, consecrated men and women, seminarians and committed lay persons, may the Blessed Virgin Mary guide us. With her and like her, we are free so as to be saints; free so as to be poor, chaste, and obedient; free for all because detached from all, free from self so that others may grow in Christ, the true Holy One of the Father and the Shepherd to whom priests, as his presence, lend their voice and their gestures; free to bring to today's world Jesus who died and rose again, Jesus who remains with us until the end of time and who gives himself to all in the Most Holy Eucharist.

10. *Called by Name*

From *Lectio Divina by His Holiness Benedict XVI*, Visit to the Pontifical Roman Major Seminary on the Memorial of Our Lady of Trust, March 4, 2011

I am very glad to be here at least once a year with my seminarians, with the young men bound for the priesthood to form the future presbyterate of Rome. I am delighted that this happens every year on the day of Our Lady of Trust, the Mother who day after day accompanies us with her love and gives us the confidence to journey on toward Christ.

"In the unity of the Spirit" is the theme that guides your reflections during this year of formation. It is an expression found, precisely, in the passage of the Letter to the Ephesians that has been presented to us, in which St. Paul begs the members of that community to "maintain the unity of the Spirit" (Eph 4:3). The second part of the Letter to the Ephesians begins with this text, the so-called "paranetical" or exhortatory part, and begins with the word *"parakalo,"* "I beg you." However, the same word, *"Paraklitos,"* also comes at the end, thus it is an exhortation in the light, in the power of the Holy Spirit. The Apostle's exhortation is based on the mystery of salvation that he had presented in the first three chapters. In fact, our passage begins with the word "therefore": "I *therefore* ... beg you ..." (Eph 4:1).

The behavior of Christians is the consequence of the gift, the realization of all that is given to us, every day. Yet, if it is simply the realization of the gift given to us it is not an automatic effect, because with God we are always in the reality of freedom hence—since the response and also the realization of the gift is freedom—the Apostle must recall it, he cannot take it for granted. Baptism, as we know, does not automatically produce a consistent life: this is the fruit of the will and of the persevering commitment to collaborate with the gift, with the Grace received. And this commitment costs us effort; there is a price to pay in person. This may be why St. Paul refers here to his actual condition: "I therefore, a *prisoner* for the Lord, beg you ..." (Eph 4:1).

Following Christ means sharing in his Passion, his Cross, following him to the very end, and this participation in the Teacher's destiny profoundly unites us to him and reinforces the authoritativeness of the Apostle's exhortation.

We now reach the heart of our meditation, encountering a particularly striking word: "call," "vocation." St. Paul wrote, "lead a life worthy of the *calling*, of the *klesis* to which you have been called" (Eph 4:1). And he was to repeat it a little later, affirming that "you were *called* to the one hope that belongs to your *call*" (Eph 4:4). Here, in this case, it is a question of the vocation common to all Christians—namely, the baptismal vocation, the call to be in Christ and to live in him, in his Body. In these words an experience is inscribed, and the echo resounds of that of the first disciples, which we know from the Gospels: when Jesus passed along the shores of the Sea of Galilee and called Simon and Andrew, then James and John (cf. Mk 1:16–20); and even earlier, at the River Jordan after his Baptism, when, noticing that Andrew and the other disciple were following him Jesus said to them, "Come and see" (Jn 1:39). Christian life begins with a call and always remains an answer, to the very end. And this is in the dimension of believing and that of doing: both the faith and the behavior of the Christian correspond to the grace of the vocation.

I spoke of the call of the first Apostles, but the word "call" reminds us above all of the Mother of every call, of Mary Most Holy, the Chosen One, the One Called par excellence. The image of the Annunciation to Mary portrays far more than that particular Gospel episode, despite its fundamental character: it contains the whole mystery of Mary, the whole of her history, of her being; and at the same time it speaks of the Church, of her essence as it has always been, as well as of every individual believer in Christ, of every Christian soul who is called.

At this point we must bear in mind that we are not speaking of people of the past. God, the Lord, has called each one of us, each one is called by name. God is so great that he has time for each one of us, he knows me, he knows each one of us by name, personally. It is a personal call for each one of us. I think we should meditate time and again on this mystery: God, the Lord, has called me, is calling me, knows me, awaits my answer just as he awaited Mary's answer and the answer of the Apostles. God calls me: this fact must make us attentive to God's voice, attentive to his word, to his call for me, in order to respond, in order to realize this part of the history of salvation for which he has called me.

Then, in this text, St. Paul points out to us several concrete elements of this answer with four words: "lowliness," "meekness," "patience," "forbearing one another in love" (cf. Eph 4:2). Perhaps we could meditate briefly on these words in which the Christian journey is expressed. Then at the end, we shall once again return to this.

"Lowliness": the Greek word is *"tapeinophrosyne,"* the same word that St. Paul uses in his Letter to the Philippians when he speaks of the Lord who was God and who humbled himself; he made himself *"tapeinos,"* he descended to the point of making himself a creature, of making himself man, obedient even unto death on the Cross (cf. Phil 2:7–8). Lowliness, then, is not just any word, any kind of modesty, something ... it is a Christological word. Imitating God who descends even to me, who is so great that he makes himself my friend, suffers for me, and dies for me. This is the humility we must learn: God's humility. It means that we must always see ourselves in God's light; thus, at the same time, we can know the greatness of being a person loved by God but also our own smallness, our poverty, and thus behave correctly, not as masters but as servants. As St. Paul says, "Not that we lord it over your faith; we work with you for your joy" (2 Cor 1:24). Being a priest, even more than being a Christian, implies this humility.

"Meekness": the Greek text uses here the word *"praütes,"* the same word that appears in the Beatitudes: "Blessed are the meek, for they shall inherit the earth" (Mt 5:5). And in the Book of Numbers, the fourth Book of Moses, we find the affirmation that Moses was the meekest man in the world (cf. Nm 12:3), and in this sense he was a prefiguration of Christ, of Jesus, who said of himself, "I am gentle and lowly in heart" (Mt 11:29). So this word "meek," or "gentle," is also a Christological word and once again implies imitating Christ in this manner. For in Baptism we are configured to Christ so we must configure ourselves to Christ, we must discover this spirit of being meek, without violence, of convincing with love and kindness.

"Patience" [magnanimity], "*makrothymia*," means generosity of heart, it means not being minimalists who give only what is strictly necessary: let us give ourselves with all that we possess and we will also increase in magnanimity.

"Forbearing one another in love": it is a daily duty to tolerate one another in our own otherness and precisely to tolerate one another with humility, to learn true love.

And let us now take a step further. This word "call" is followed by the ecclesial dimension. We have now spoken of the vocation as a very personal call: God calls me, knows me, waits for my personal response. However, at the same time God's call is a call to a community, it is an ecclesial call. God calls us to a community. It is true that in this passage on which we are meditating the word "*ekklesia*," "Church," is not found, but the reality is all the more evident. St. Paul speaks of a Spirit and a body. The Spirit creates the body and unites us as it were in one body. And then he speaks of unity, he speaks of the chain of being, of the bond of peace. And with these words he refers to the word "prisoner" (Eph 4:1) at the beginning: it is always the same word, "I am in chains," "chains will bind you," but behind them is the great, invisible, liberating chain of love.

We are in this bond of peace that is the Church, it is the great bond that unites us to Christ. Perhaps we must also meditate personally on this point: we are called personally, but we are called to a body. And this is not something abstract but is very real.

At this time the Seminary is the body in which your being on a common journey is brought about in practice. Then there will be the parish: accepting, supporting, enlivening the whole parish, the people, those who are likable and those who are not, becoming integrated into this body. Body: the Church is a body so she has structures, she really has a law, and this time it is not so simple to integrate. Of course, we want the personal relationship with God, but we often do not like the body. Yet in this very way we are in communion with Christ: by accepting this corporeity of his Church, of the Spirit who is incarnate in the body.

However, perhaps we frequently feel the problem, the difficulty of this community, starting from the actual community of the Seminary to the large community of the Church, with her institutions. We must also keep in mind that it is really lovely to be in a company, to journey on in a large company of all the centuries, to have friends in Heaven and on earth and to be aware of the beauty of this body, to be happy that the Lord has called us in a body and has given us friends in all the parts of the world.

I said that the word *"ekklesia"* is not found here, but there is the word "body," the word "Spirit," the word "bond," and in this brief passage the word "one" recurs seven times. Thus we feel that the Apostle has the unity of the Church at heart. And he ends with a "scale of unity," until Unity: God is One, the God of all. God is One, and the oneness of God is expressed in our communion, because God is the Father, the Creator of us all, and so we are all brothers and sisters, we are all one body, and the oneness of God is the condition for and also the creation of human brotherhood, of peace. Let us therefore also meditate on this mystery of oneness and the importance of always seeking oneness in the communion of the one Christ, of the one God.

We may now go a step further. If we ask ourselves what the deep meaning of this use of the word "call" is, we see that it is one of the doors that open on to the Trinitarian mystery. So far we have spoken of the mystery of the Church of the one God, but the Trinitarian mystery also appears. Jesus is the mediator of the call of the Father that happens through the Holy Spirit.

The Christian vocation cannot but have a Trinitarian form, both at the level of the individual person and at the level of the ecclesial community. The mystery of the Church is enlivened throughout by the dynamism of the Holy Spirit, which is a vocational dynamism in the broad and perennial sense, starting with Abraham who was the first to hear God's call and to respond with faith and action (cf. Gen 12:1–3), until the "behold" of Mary, a perfect reflection of that of the Son of God at the moment when he accepted the Father's call to come into the world (cf. Heb 10:5–7).

Thus, at the "heart" of the Church—as St. Thérèse of the Child Jesus would say—the call of every individual Christian is a Trinitarian mystery: the mystery of the encounter with Jesus, with the Word made flesh, through whom God the Father calls us to communion with him and for this reason wishes to give us his Holy Spirit; and it is precisely through the Spirit that we can respond authentically to Jesus and to the Father within a real, filial relationship. Without the breath of the Holy Spirit the Christian vocation simply cannot be explained, it loses its vitality.

And finally the last passage. The form of unity according to the Spirit, as I said, calls for the imitation of Jesus, configuration to him in the concreteness of his behavior. The Apostle writes, as in our meditation: "with all lowliness and meekness, with patience, forbearing one another in love," and then adds that the unity of the Spirit should be maintained "in the bond of peace" (Eph 4:2–3).

The unity of the Church does not come from a "mold" imposed from the outside; rather, it is the fruit of a harmony, a common commitment to behave like Jesus, by virtue of his Spirit.

St. John Chrysostom made a very fine commentary on this passage. Chrysostom comments on the image of the "bond," the "bond of peace." He says, "a glorious bond is this; with this bond let us bind ourselves together with one another and unto God. This is a bond that bruises not, nor cramps the hands it binds, but it leaves them free, and gives them ample play and greater courage."[40]

Here we find the evangelical paradox: Christian love is a bond, as we said, but a liberating bond! The image of the bond, as I told you, brings us back to the situation of St. Paul who is a "prisoner" and is "in chains." The Apostle is in chains because of the Lord, just as Jesus made himself a servant to set us free. If we are to maintain the unity of the Spirit we must impress upon our own behavior that humility, meekness, and patience to which Jesus witnessed in his Passion; it is necessary to have hand and heart bound by the bond of love that he himself accepted for us by making himself our servant. This is the "bond

40. John Chrysostom, *Commentary on the Epistle to the Galatians: And Homilies on the Epistle to the Ephesians*, trans. William John Copeland (London: J. G. F. and J. Rivington, 1840), 208.

of peace." And St. John Chrysostom says further in the same commentary, "if you would attach yourself to another [your brother] ... these thus bound by love bear all things with ease ... thus also here he would have us tied one to another; not simply that we be at peace, not simply that we love one another [to be friends], but that all should be one, one soul"[41]

The Pauline text, a few elements of which we have meditated on, is very rich. I have only been able to convey to you a few ideas, which I entrust to your meditation. And let us pray the Virgin Mary, Our Lady of Trust, to help us walk joyfully in the unity of the Spirit. Thank you!

11. *Follow Me*

From *Message of the Holy Father for the 48th World Day of Prayer for Vocations*, May 15, 2011

The 48th World Day of Prayer for Vocations, to be celebrated on May 15, 2011, the Fourth Sunday of Easter, invites us to reflect on the theme "Proposing Vocations in the Local Church." Seventy years ago, Venerable Pius XII established the Pontifical Work of Priestly Vocations. Similar bodies, led by priests and members of the lay faithful, were subsequently established by Bishops in many dioceses as a response to the call of the Good Shepherd who, "when he saw the crowds, had compassion on them, because they were like sheep without a shepherd," and went on to say, "The harvest is plentiful but the laborers are

41. Ibid., 207.

few. Pray therefore the Lord of the harvest to send out laborers into his harvest!" (Mt 9:36–38).

The work of carefully encouraging and supporting vocations finds a radiant source of inspiration in those places in the Gospel where Jesus calls his disciples to follow him and trains them with love and care. We should pay close attention to the way that Jesus called his closest associates to proclaim the Kingdom of God (cf. Lk 10:9). In the first place, it is clear that the first thing he did was to pray for them: before calling them, Jesus spent the night alone in prayer, listening to the will of the Father (cf. Lk 6:12) in a spirit of interior detachment from mundane concerns. It is Jesus' intimate conversation with the Father that results in the calling of his disciples. Vocations to the ministerial priesthood and to the consecrated life are first and foremost the fruit of constant contact with the living God and insistent prayer lifted up to the "Lord of the harvest," whether in parish communities, in Christian families, or in groups specifically devoted to prayer for vocations.

At the beginning of his public life, the Lord called some fishermen on the shore of the Sea of Galilee: "Follow me and I will make you fishers of men" (Mt 4:19). He revealed his messianic mission to them by the many signs that showed his love for humanity and the gift of the Father's mercy. Through his words and his way of life he prepared them to carry on his saving work. Finally, knowing "that his hour had come to depart out of this world to the Father" (Jn 13:1), he entrusted to them the memorial of his death and resurrection, and before ascending into heaven he sent them out to the whole world with the command "Go, therefore, make disciples of all nations" (Mt 28:19).

It is a challenging and uplifting invitation that Jesus addresses to those to whom he says, "Follow me!" He invites them to
become his friends, to listen attentively to his word, and to live
with him. He teaches them complete commitment to God and
to the extension of his kingdom in accordance with the law of
the Gospel: "Unless a grain of wheat falls into the earth and dies,
it remains alone; but if it dies, it bears much fruit" (Jn 12:24).
He invites them to leave behind their own narrow agenda and
their notions of self-fulfillment in order to immerse themselves
in another will, the will of God, and to be guided by it. He gives
them an experience of fraternity, one born of that total openness to God (cf. Mt 12:49–50), that becomes the hallmark of the
community of Jesus: "By this everyone will know that you are
my disciples, if you have love for one another" (Jn 13:35).

It is no less challenging to follow Christ today. It means
learning to keep our gaze fixed on Jesus, growing close to him,
listening to his word, and encountering him in the sacraments;
it means learning to conform our will to his. This requires a
genuine school of formation for all those who would prepare
themselves for the ministerial priesthood or the consecrated life
under the guidance of the competent ecclesial authorities. The
Lord does not fail to call people at every stage of life to share in
his mission and to serve the Church in the ordained ministry
and in the consecrated life. The Church is "called to safeguard
this gift, to esteem it and love it. She is responsible for the birth
and development of priestly vocations."[42] Particularly in these
times, when the voice of the Lord seems to be drowned out by

---

42. Pope John Paul II, Apostolic Exhortation *Pastores Dabo Vobis*, no. 41.

"other voices" and his invitation to follow him by the gift of one's own life may seem too difficult, every Christian community, every member of the Church, needs consciously to feel responsibility for promoting vocations. It is important to encourage and support those who show clear signs of a call to priestly life and religious consecration and to enable them to feel the warmth of the whole community as they respond "yes" to God and the Church. I encourage them, in the same words that I addressed to those who have already chosen to enter the seminary: "You have done a good thing. Because people will always have need of God, even in an age marked by technical mastery of the world and globalization: they will always need the God who has revealed himself in Jesus Christ, the God who gathers us together in the universal Church in order to learn with him and through him life's true meaning and in order to uphold and apply the standards of true humanity."[43]

It is essential that every local Church become more sensitive and attentive to the pastoral care of vocations, helping children and young people in particular at every level of family, parish, and associations—as Jesus did with his disciples—to grow into a genuine and affectionate friendship with the Lord, cultivated through personal and liturgical prayer; to grow in familiarity with the Sacred Scriptures and thus to listen attentively and fruitfully to the word of God; to understand that entering into God's will does not crush or destroy a person, but instead leads to the discovery of the deepest truth about ourselves; and finally to be generous and fraternal in relationships with others, since

---

43. Pope Benedict XVI, *Letter to Seminarians*, October 18, 2010.

it is only in being open to the love of God that we discover true joy and the fulfillment of our aspirations. "Proposing Vocations in the Local Church" means having the courage, through an attentive and suitable concern for vocations, to point out this challenging way of following Christ that, because it is so rich in meaning, is capable of engaging the whole of one's life.

I address a particular word to you, my dear brother Bishops. To ensure the continuity and growth of your saving mission in Christ, you should "foster priestly and religious vocations as much as possible, and should take a special interest in missionary vocations."[44] The Lord needs you to cooperate with him in ensuring that his call reaches the hearts of those whom he has chosen. Choose carefully those who work in the Diocesan Vocations Office, that valuable means for the promotion and organization of the pastoral care of vocations and the prayer that sustains it and guarantees its effectiveness. I would also remind you, dear brother Bishops, of the concern of the universal Church for an equitable distribution of priests in the world. Your openness to the needs of dioceses experiencing a dearth of vocations will become a blessing from God for your communities and a sign to the faithful of a priestly service that generously considers the needs of the entire Church.

The Second Vatican Council explicitly reminded us that "the duty of fostering vocations pertains to the whole Christian community, which should exercise it above all by a fully Christian life."[45] I wish, then, to say a special word of acknowledgment and encouragement to those who work closely in various ways

---

44. Cf. Second Vatican Council, Decree *Christus Dominus* (October 28, 1965), no. 15.
45. Ibid., no. 2.

with the priests in their parishes. In particular, I turn to those who can offer a specific contribution to the pastoral care of vocations: to priests, families, catechists, and leaders of parish groups. I ask priests to testify to their communion with their bishop and their fellow priests, and thus to provide a rich soil for the seeds of a priestly vocation. May families be "animated by the spirit of faith and love and by the sense of duty" that is capable of helping children to welcome generously the call to priesthood and to religious life.[46] May catechists and leaders of Catholic groups and ecclesial movements, convinced of their educational mission, seek to "guide the young people entrusted to them so that these will recognize and freely accept a divine vocation."[47]

Dear brothers and sisters, your commitment to the promotion and care of vocations becomes most significant and pastorally effective when carried out in the unity of the Church and in the service of communion. For this reason, every moment in the life of the Church community—catechesis, formation meetings, liturgical prayer, pilgrimages—can be a precious opportunity for awakening in the People of God, and in particular in children and young people, a sense of belonging to the Church and of responsibility for answering the call to priesthood and to religious life by a free and informed decision.

The ability to foster vocations is a hallmark of the vitality of a local Church. With trust and perseverance let us invoke the aid of the Virgin Mary, that by the example of her own acceptance of God's saving plan and her powerful intercession, every

46. Cf. Second Vatican Council, Decree *Optatam Totius* (October 28, 1965), no. 2.
47. Cf. ibid.

community will be more and more open to saying "yes" to the Lord who is constantly calling new laborers to his harvest. With this hope, I cordially impart to all my Apostolic Blessing.

12. *The Faithfulness of God*

From *Message of the Holy Father for the 50th World Day of Prayer for Vocations*, April 21, 2013

On the occasion of the 50th World Day of Prayer for Vocations, to be held on April 21, 2013, the Fourth Sunday of Easter, I want to invite you to reflect on the theme *"Vocations as a sign of hope founded in faith,"* which happily occurs during the Year of Faith, the year marking the fiftieth anniversary of the opening of the Second Vatican Council. While the Council was in session, the Servant of God, Paul VI, instituted this day of worldwide prayer to God the Father, asking him to continue to send workers for his Church (cf. Mt 9:38). "The problem of having a sufficient number of priests," as the Pope stated at the time, "has an immediate impact on all of the faithful: not simply because they depend on it for the religious future of Christian society, but also because this problem is the precise and inescapable indicator of the vitality of faith and love of individual parish and diocesan communities and the evidence of the moral health of Christian families. Wherever numerous vocations to the priesthood and consecrated life are to be found, that is where people are living the Gospel with generosity."[48]

---

48. Pope Paul VI, *Radio Message* (April 11, 1964).

During the intervening decades, the various Christian communities all over the world have gathered each year on the Fourth Sunday of Easter, united in prayer, to ask from God the gift of holy vocations and to propose once again, for the reflection of all, the urgent need to respond to the divine call. Indeed, this significant annual event has fostered a strong commitment to placing the importance of vocations to the priesthood and the consecrated life ever more at the center of the spirituality, prayer, and pastoral action of the faithful.

Hope is the expectation of something positive in the future, yet at the same time it must sustain our present existence, which is often marked by dissatisfaction and failures. On what is our hope founded? Looking at the history of the people of Israel, recounted in the Old Testament, we see one element that constantly emerges, especially in times of particular difficulty like the time of the Exile, an element found especially in the writings of the prophets, namely remembrance of God's promises to the Patriarchs: a remembrance that invites us to imitate the exemplary attitude of Abraham, who, as Saint Paul reminds us, "believed, hoping against hope, that he would become 'the father of many nations,' according to what was said, 'Thus shall your descendants be'" (Rom 4:18). One consoling and enlightening truth that emerges from the whole of salvation history, then, is God's faithfulness to the covenant that he entered into, renewing it whenever man infringed it through infidelity and sin, from the time of the flood (cf. Gen 8:21–22) to that of the Exodus and the journey through the desert (cf. Dt 9:7). That same faithfulness led him to seal the new and eternal covenant with man, through the blood of his Son, who died and rose again for our salvation.

At every moment, especially the most difficult ones, the Lord's faithfulness is always the authentic driving force of salvation history, which arouses the hearts of men and women and confirms them in the hope of one day reaching the "promised land." This is where we find the sure foundation of every hope: God never abandons us, and he remains true to his word. For that reason, in every situation, whether positive or negative, we can nourish a firm hope and pray with the psalmist: "Only in God can my soul find rest; my hope comes from him" (Ps 62:6). To have hope, therefore, is the equivalent of trusting in God who is faithful, who keeps the promises of the covenant. Faith and hope, then, are closely related. "Hope" in fact is a key word in biblical faith, to the extent that in certain passages the words "faith" and "hope" seem to be interchangeable. In this way, the Letter to the Hebrews makes a direct connection between the "unwavering profession of hope" (10:23) and the "fullness of faith" (10:22). Similarly, when the First Letter of Saint Peter exhorts the Christians to be always ready to give an account of the "logos"—the meaning and rationale—of their hope (cf. 3:15), "hope" is the equivalent of "faith."[49]

Dear Brothers and Sisters, what exactly is God's faithfulness, to which we adhere with unwavering hope? It is his love! He, the Father, pours his love into our innermost self through the Holy Spirit (cf. Rom 5:5). And this love, fully manifested in Jesus Christ, engages with our existence and demands a response in terms of what each individual wants to do with his or her life and what he or she is prepared to offer in order to live it to the

---

49. Pope Benedict XVI, Encyclical Letter *Spe Salvi*, no. 2.

full. The love of God sometimes follows paths one could never have imagined, but it always reaches those who are willing to be found. Hope is nourished, then, by this certainty: "We ourselves have known and believed in the love that God has for us" (1 Jn 4:16). This deep, demanding love, which penetrates well below the surface, gives us courage; it gives us hope in our life's journey and in our future; it makes us trust in ourselves, in history, and in other people. I want to speak particularly to the young, and I say to you once again: "What would your life be without this love? God takes care of men and women from creation to the end of time, when he will bring his plan of salvation to completion. In the Risen Lord we have the certainty of our hope!"[50]

Just as he did during his earthly existence, so today the risen Jesus walks along the streets of our life and sees us immersed in our activities, with all our desires and our needs. In the midst of our everyday circumstances he continues to speak to us; he calls us to live our life with him, for only he is capable of satisfying our thirst for hope. He lives now among the community of disciples that is the Church, and still today calls people to follow him. The call can come at any moment. Today too, Jesus continues to say, "Come, follow me" (Mk 10:21). Accepting his invitation means no longer choosing our own path. Following him means immersing our own will in the will of Jesus, truly giving him priority, giving him pride of place in every area of our lives: in the family, at work, in our personal interests, in ourselves. It

50. Pope Benedict XVI, *Address to the Young People of the Diocese of San Marino-Montefeltro*, Pastoral Visit to the Diocese of San Marino-Montefeltro, Pennabilli, June 19, 2011.

means handing over our very lives to him, living in profound intimacy with him, entering through him into communion with the Father in the Holy Spirit, and consequently with our brothers and sisters. This communion of life with Jesus is the privileged "setting" in which we can experience hope and in which life will be full and free.

Vocations to the priesthood and the consecrated life are born out of the experience of a personal encounter with Christ, out of sincere and confident dialogue with him, so as to enter into his will. It is necessary, therefore, to grow in the experience of faith, understood as a profound relationship with Jesus, as inner attentiveness to his voice that is heard deep within us. This process, which enables us to respond positively to God's call, is possible in Christian communities where the faith is lived intensely, where generous witness is given of adherence to the Gospel, where there is a strong sense of mission that leads people to make the total gift of self for the Kingdom of God, nourished by recourse to the Sacraments, especially the Eucharist, and by a fervent life of prayer. This latter "must on the one hand be something very personal, an encounter between my intimate self and God, the living God. On the other hand it must be constantly guided and enlightened by the great prayers of the Church and of the saints, by liturgical prayer, in which the Lord teaches us again and again how to pray properly."[51]

Deep and constant prayer brings about growth in the faith of the Christian community, in the unceasingly renewed certainty that God never abandons his people and that he sustains

51. Pope Benedict XVI, Encyclical Letter *Spe Salvi*, no. 34.

them by raising up particular vocations—to the priesthood and the consecrated life—so that they can be signs of hope for the world. Indeed, priests and religious are called to give themselves unconditionally to the People of God, in a service of love for the Gospel and the Church, serving that firm hope that can only come from an openness to the divine. By means of the witness of their faith and apostolic zeal, therefore, they can transmit, especially to the younger generations, a strong desire to respond generously and promptly to Christ who calls them to follow him more closely. Whenever a disciple of Jesus accepts the divine call to dedicate himself to the priestly ministry or to the consecrated life, we witness one of the most mature fruits of the Christian community, which helps us to look with particular trust and hope to the future of the Church and to her commitment to evangelization. This constantly requires new workers to preach the Gospel, to celebrate the Eucharist and the Sacrament of Reconciliation. So let there be committed priests, who know how to accompany young people as "companions on the journey," helping them, on life's often tortuous and difficult path, to recognize Christ, the Way, the Truth, and the Life (cf. Jn 14:6), telling them, with Gospel courage, how beautiful it is to serve God, the Christian community, one's brothers and sisters. Let there be priests who manifest the fruitfulness of an enthusiastic commitment, which gives a sense of completeness to their lives, because it is founded on faith in him who loved us first (cf. 1 Jn 4:19).

Equally, I hope that young people, who are presented with so many superficial and ephemeral options, will be able to cultivate a desire for what is truly worthy, for lofty objectives, radical choices, service to others in imitation of Jesus. Dear young people, do not be afraid to follow him and to walk the demanding and courageous paths of charity and generous commitment! In that way you will be happy to serve, you will be witnesses of a joy that the world cannot give, you will be living flames of an infinite and eternal love, you will learn to "give an account of the hope that is within you!" (1 Pt 3:15).

PART 2

ROOTED IN LOVE

13. *A Journey of Love*

From *Address of His Holiness Pope Benedict XVI, Meeting with Seminarians*, Apostolic Journey to Cologne on the Occasion of the 20th World Youth Day, August 19, 2005

You are seminarians, that is to say, young people devoting an intense period of your lives to seeking a personal relationship with Christ, an encounter with him, in preparation for your important mission in the Church. This is what a seminary is: more than a place, it is a significant time in the life of a follower of Jesus.

I can imagine the echo that resounds in your hearts from the words of the theme of this 20th World Youth Day—*"We have come to worship him"*—and the entire moving narration of the searching and finding of the Wise Men. Each in his own way—we consider the three witnesses we have just heard—like them, they see a star, set out on their journey, they too must face what is unclear and are able to arrive at their destination under God's guidance.

This evangelical passage of the Wise Men who search out and find Jesus has a special meaning precisely for you, dear seminarians, because you are on an authentic journey, engaged in discerning—and this is a true journey—and confirming your call to the priesthood. Let us pause and reflect on this theme.

Why did the Magi set off from afar to go to Bethlehem? The

answer has to do with the mystery of the "star" that they saw "in the East" and that they recognized as the star of the "King of the Jews," that is to say, the sign of the birth of the Messiah (cf. Mt 2:2). So their journey was inspired by a powerful hope, strengthened and guided by the star, which led them toward the King of the Jews, toward the kingship of God himself. This is the meaning behind our journey: to serve the kingship of God in the world.

The Magi set out because of a deep desire that prompted them to leave everything and begin a journey. It was as though they had always been waiting for that star. It was as if the journey had always been a part of their destiny and was finally about to begin.

Dear friends, this is the mystery of God's call, the mystery of vocation. It is part of the life of every Christian, but it is particularly evident in those whom Christ asks to leave everything in order to follow him more closely.

The seminarian experiences the beauty of that call in a moment of grace that could be defined as "falling in love." His soul is filled with amazement, which makes him ask in prayer, "Lord, why me?" But love knows no "why"; it is a free gift to which one responds with the gift of self.

The seminary years are devoted to formation and discernment. Formation, as you well know, has different strands that converge in the unity of the person: it includes human, spiritual, and cultural dimensions. Its deepest goal is to bring the student to an intimate knowledge of the God who has revealed his face in Jesus Christ.

For this, in-depth study of Sacred Scripture is needed, and

also of the faith and life of the Church in which the Scripture dwells as the Word of life. This must all be linked with the questions prompted by our reason and with the broader context of modern life.

Such study can at times seem arduous, but it is an indispensable part of our encounter with Christ and our vocation to proclaim him. All this is aimed at shaping a steady and balanced personality, one capable of receiving validly and fulfilling responsibly the priestly mission.

The role of formators is decisive: the quality of the presbyterate in a particular Church depends greatly on that of the seminary and consequently on the quality of those responsible for formation.

Dear seminarians, for this very reason we pray today with genuine gratitude for your superiors, professors, and educators, who are spiritually present at this meeting. Let us ask the Lord to help them carry out as well as possible the important task entrusted to them.

The seminary years are a time of journeying, of exploration, but above all of discovering Christ. It is only when a young man has had a personal experience of Christ that he can truly understand the Lord's will and consequently his own vocation.

The better you know Jesus the more his mystery attracts you. The more you discover him, the more you are moved to seek him. This is a movement of the Spirit that lasts throughout life and that makes the seminary a time of immense promise, a true "springtime."

When the Magi came to Bethlehem, "going into the house they saw the child with Mary his mother, and they fell down and worshiped him" (Mt 2:11). Here at last was the long-awaited moment: their encounter with Jesus.

"Going into the house": this house in some sense represents the Church. In order to find the Savior, one has to enter the house, which is the Church.

During his time in the seminary, a particularly important process of maturation takes place in the consciousness of the young seminarian: he no longer sees the Church "from the outside," but rather, as it were, "from the inside," and he comes to sense that she is his "home," inasmuch as she is the home of Christ, where "Mary his mother" dwells.

It is Mary who shows him Jesus her Son; she introduces him and in a sense enables him to see and touch Jesus and to take him into his arms. Mary teaches the seminarian to contemplate Jesus with the eyes of the heart and to make Jesus his very life.

Each moment of seminary life can be an opportunity for loving experience of the presence of Our Lady, who introduces everyone to an encounter with Christ in the silence of meditation, prayer, and fraternity. Mary helps us to meet the Lord above all in the celebration of the Eucharist, when, in the Word and in the consecrated Bread, he becomes our daily spiritual nourishment.

"They fell down and worshiped him ... and offered him gifts: gold, frankincense and myrrh" (Mt 2:11-12). Here is the culmination of the whole journey: encounter becomes adoration; it blossoms into an act of faith and love that acknowledges in Jesus, born of Mary, the Son of God made man.

How can we fail to see prefigured in this gesture of the Magi the faith of Simon Peter and of the other Apostles, the faith of

Paul and of all the saints, particularly of the many saintly seminarians and priests who have graced the two thousand years of the Church's history?

The secret of holiness is friendship with Christ and faithful obedience to his will. St. Ambrose said, "Christ is everything for us"; and St. Benedict warned against putting anything before the love of Christ.

May Christ be everything for you, Dear seminarians, be the first to offer him what is most precious to you, as Pope John Paul II suggested in his Message for this World Youth Day: the gold of your freedom, the incense of your ardent prayer, the myrrh of your most profound affection.[1]

The seminary years are a time of preparing for mission. The Magi "departed for their own country" and most certainly bore witness to their encounter with the King of the Jews.

You too, after your long, necessary program of seminary formation, will be sent forth as ministers of Christ; indeed, each of you will return as an *alter Christus*.

On their homeward journey, the Magi surely had to deal with dangers, weariness, disorientation, doubts. The star was no longer there to guide them! The light was now within them. Their task was to guard and nourish it in the constant memory of Christ, of his Holy Face, of his ineffable Love.

Dear seminarians! One day, God willing, by the consecration of the Holy Spirit you too will begin your mission. Remember always the words of Jesus: "Abide in my love" (Jn 15:9). If you abide close to Christ, with Christ, and in Christ, you will bear

---

1. Cf. Pope John Paul II, *Message for the Twentieth World Youth Day* (August 6, 2005), no. 4.

much fruit, just as he promised. You have not chosen him—we have just heard this in the witnesses given—, he has chosen you (cf. Jn 15:16).

Here is the secret of your vocation and your mission! It is kept in the Immaculate Heart of Mary, who watches over each one of you with a mother's love. Have recourse to Mary, often and with confidence.

I assure you of my affection and my daily prayers. And I bless all of you from my heart.

14. *Called to Communion*

From *Message of His Holiness Pope Benedict XVI for the 44th World Day of Prayer for Vocations*, April 29, 2007

The annual World Day of Prayer for Vocations is an appropriate occasion for highlighting the importance of vocations in the life and mission of the Church, as well as for intensifying our prayer that they may increase in number and quality. For the coming celebration, I would like to draw the attention of the whole people of God to the following theme, which is more topical than ever: *the vocation to the service of the Church as communion.*

Last year, in the Wednesday general audiences, I began a new series of catechesis dedicated to the relationship between Christ and the Church. I pointed out that the first Christian community was built, in its original core, when some fishermen of Galilee, having met Jesus, let themselves be conquered by his gaze and his voice and accepted his pressing invitation: "Follow me and I will make you become fishers of men!" (Mk 1:17; cf. Mt 4:19). In fact, God has always chosen some individuals to work with him in a more direct way, in order to accomplish his plan of salvation. In the Old Testament, in the beginning, he called Abraham to form a "great nation" (Gen 12:2); afterward, he called Moses to free Israel from the slavery of Egypt (cf. Ex 3:10). Subsequently, he designated other persons, especially the prophets, to defend and keep alive the covenant with his people. In the New Testament, Jesus, the promised Messiah, invited each of the Apostles to be with him (cf. Mk 3:14) and to share his mission. At the Last Supper, while entrusting them with the duty of perpetuating the memorial of his death and resurrection until his glorious return at the end of time, he offered for them to his Father this heartbroken prayer: "I made known to them your name, and I will make it known, that the love with which you have loved me may be in them, and I in them" (Jn 17:26). The mission of the Church, therefore, is founded on an intimate and faithful communion with God.

The Second Vatican Council's Constitution *Lumen Gentium* describes the Church as "a people made one with the unity of the Father, the Son and the Holy Spirit,"[2] in which is reflected the very mystery of God. This means that the love of the Trinity is reflected in her. Moreover, thanks to the work of the Holy Spirit, all the members of the Church form "one body and one spirit" in Christ. This people, organically structured under the guidance of its Pastors, lives the mystery of communion with God and with the brethren, especially when it gathers for the

2. Cf. Second Vatican Council, *Lumen Gentium*, no. 4.

Eucharist. The Eucharist is the source of that ecclesial unity for which Jesus prayed on the eve of his passion: "Father ... that they also may be one in us, so that the world may believe that you have sent me" (Jn 17:21). This intense communion favors the growth of generous vocations at the service of the Church: the heart of the believer, filled with divine love, is moved to dedicate itself wholly to the cause of the Kingdom. In order to foster vocations, therefore, it is important that pastoral activity be attentive to the mystery of the Church as communion; because whoever lives in an ecclesial community that is harmonious, co-responsible and conscientious, certainly learns more easily to discern the call of the Lord. The care of vocations, therefore, demands a constant education for listening to the voice of God. This is what Eli did when he helped the young Samuel to understand what God was asking of him and to put it immediately into action (cf. 1 Sm 3:9). Now, docile and faithful listening can only take place in a climate of intimate communion with God that is realized principally in prayer. According to the explicit command of the Lord, we must implore the gift of vocations, in the first place by praying untiringly and together to the "Lord of the harvest." The invitation is in the plural: "Therefore pray the Lord of the harvest to send out laborers into his harvest" (Mt 9:38). This invitation of the Lord corresponds well with the style of the "Our Father," (Mt 6:9) the prayer that he taught us and that constitutes a "synthesis of the whole Gospel,"[3] according to the well-known expression of Tertullian. In this perspective, yet another expression of Jesus is instructive: "If two of you

---

3. Cf. Tertullian, *De Oratione* 1.6.

agree on earth about anything they ask, it will be done for them
by my Father in heaven" (Mt 18:19). The Good Shepherd, therefore, invites us to pray to the heavenly Father, to pray unitedly
and insistently, that he may send vocations for the service of the
Church as communion.

Harvesting the pastoral experience of past centuries, the
Second Vatican Council highlighted the importance of educating future priests to an authentic ecclesial communion. In this
regard, we read in *Presbyterorum Ordinis*, "Exercising the office
of Christ, the shepherd and head, according to their share of
his authority, the priests, in the name of the Bishop, gather the
family of God together as a brotherhood enlivened by one spirit.
Through Christ they lead them in the Holy Spirit to God the
Father."[4] The post-synodal Apostolic Exhortation *Pastores Dabo
Vobis* echoes this statement of the Council when it underlines
that the priest is "the servant of the Church as communion because—in union with the Bishop and closely related to the presbyterate—he builds up the unity of the Church community in
harmony of diverse vocations, charisms and services."[5] It is indispensable that, within the Christian people, every ministry
and charism be directed to full communion; and it is the duty of
the Bishop and priests to promote this communion in harmony
with every other Church vocation and service. The consecrated life, too, of its very nature, is at the service of this communion, as highlighted by my venerable predecessor John Paul II
in the post-synodal Apostolic Exhortation *Vita Consecrata*: "The

4. Cf. Second Vatican Council, Decree *Presbyterorum Ordinis* (December 7, 1965),
no. 6.

5. Cf. Pope John Paul II, Apostolic Exortation *Pastores Dabo Vobis*, no. 16.

consecrated life can certainly be credited with having effectively helped to keep alive in the Church the obligation of fraternity as a form of witness to the Trinity. By constantly promoting fraternal love, also in the form of common life, the consecrated life has shown that sharing in the Trinitarian communion can change human relationships and create a new type of solidarity."[6]

At the center of every Christian community is the Eucharist, the source and summit of the life of the Church. Whoever places himself at the service of the Gospel, if he lives the Eucharist, makes progress in love of God and neighbor and thus contributes to building the Church as communion. We can affirm that the "Eucharistic love" motivates and founds the vocational activity of the whole Church, because, as I wrote in the Encyclical *Deus Caritas Est*, vocations to the priesthood and to other ministries and services flourish within the people of God wherever there are those in whom Christ can be seen through his Word, in the sacraments, and especially in the Eucharist. This is so because "in the Church's Liturgy, in her prayer, in the living community of believers, we experience the love of God, we perceive his presence and we thus learn to recognize that presence in our daily lives. He loved us first and he continues to do so; we too, then, can respond with love."[7]

Lastly, we turn to Mary, who supported the first community where "all these with one accord devoted themselves to prayer" (Acts 1:14), so that she may help the Church in today's world to be an icon of the Trinity, an eloquent sign of divine love for all people. May the Virgin, who promptly answered the call of the

6. Cf. Pope John Paul II, Apostolic Exhortation *Vita Consecrata*, no. 41.
7. Cf. Pope Benedict XVI, Encyclical Letter *Deus Caritas Est*, no. 17.

Father saying, "Behold, I am the handmaid of the Lord," (Lk 1:38) intercede so that the Christian people will not lack servants of divine joy: priests who, in communion with their Bishops, announce the Gospel faithfully and celebrate the sacraments, take care of the people of God, and are ready to evangelize all humanity. May she ensure, also in our times, an increase in the number of consecrated persons who go against the current, living the evangelical counsels of poverty, chastity, and obedience, and give witness in a prophetic way to Christ and his liberating message of salvation. Dear brothers and sisters whom the Lord calls to particular vocations in the Church: I would like to entrust you in a special way to Mary, so that she, who more than anyone else understood the meaning of the words of Jesus, "My mother and my brethren are those who hear the word of God and do it" (Lk 8:21), may teach you to listen to her divine Son. May she help you to say with your lives, "Lo, I have come to do thy will, O God" (cf. Heb 10:7). With these wishes, I assure each one of you a special remembrance in prayer and from my heart I bless you all.

15. *For the Sake of the Kingdom of God*

From *Address of His Holiness Benedict XVI, Vespers with Priests, Religious, Deacons, and Seminarians,* Apostolic Journey to Austria, Shrine of Mariazell, September 8, 2007

We have come together in the venerable Basilica of our *Magna Mater Austriae* in Mariazell. For many generations people have come to pray here to obtain the help of the Mother of God. We too are doing the same today. We want to join Mary in

praising God's immense goodness and in expressing our gratitude to the Lord for all the blessings we have received, especially the great gift of the faith. We also wish to commend to Mary
our heartfelt concerns: to beg her protection for the Church, to
invoke her intercession for the gift of worthy vocations for Dioceses and religious communities, to implore her assistance for
families and her merciful prayers for all those longing for freedom from sin and for the grace of conversion, and, finally, to
entrust to Mary's maternal care our sick and our elderly. May
the great Mother of Austria and of Europe bring all of us to a
profound renewal of faith and life!

Dear friends, as priests, and as men and women religious,
you are servants of the mission of Jesus Christ. Just as two
thousand years ago Jesus called people to follow him, today
too young men and women are setting out at his call, attracted
by him and moved by a desire to devote their lives to serving
the Church and helping others. They have the courage to follow Christ, and they want to be his witnesses. Being a follower
of Christ is full of risks, since we are constantly threatened by
sin, lack of freedom, and defection. Consequently, we all need
his grace, just as Mary received it in its fullness. We learn to
look always, like Mary, to Christ, and to make him our criterion and measure. Thus we can participate in the universal saving mission of the Church, of which he is the head. The Lord
calls priests, religious, and lay people to go into the world, in
all its complexity, and to cooperate in the building up of God's
Kingdom. They do this in a great variety of ways: in preaching,
in building communities, in the different pastoral ministries, in
the practical exercise of charity, in research and scientific study

carried out in an apostolic spirit, in dialogue with the surrounding culture, in promoting the justice willed by God, and, in no less measure, in the recollected contemplation of the triune God and the common praise of God in their communities.

The Lord invites you to join the Church "on her pilgrim way through history." He is inviting you to become pilgrims with him and to share in his life that today too includes both the way of the Cross and the way of the Risen One through the Galilee of our existence. But he remains always one and the same Lord who, through the one Baptism, calls us to the one faith. Taking part in his journey thus means both things: the dimension of the Cross—with failure, suffering, misunderstanding, and even contempt and persecution—but also the experience of profound joy in his service and of the great consolation born of an encounter with him. Like the Church, individual parishes, communities, and all baptized Christians find in their experience of the crucified and risen Christ the source of their mission.

At the heart of the mission of Jesus Christ and of every Christian is the proclamation of the Kingdom of God. Proclaiming the Kingdom in the name of Christ means for the Church, for priests, men and women religious, and for all the baptized, a commitment to be present in the world as his witnesses. The Kingdom of God is really God himself, who makes himself present in our midst and reigns through us. The Kingdom of God is built up when God lives in us and we bring God into the world. You do so when you testify to a meaning rooted in God's creative love and opposed to every kind of meaninglessness and despair. You stand alongside all those who are earnestly striving to discover this meaning, alongside all those who want to make

something positive of their lives. By your prayer and intercession, you are the advocates of all who seek God, who are journeying toward God. You bear witness to a hope that, against
every form of hopelessness, silent or spoken, points to the fidelity and the loving concern of God. Hence you are on the side
of those who are crushed by misfortune and cannot break free
of their burdens. You bear witness to that Love that gives itself
for humanity and thus conquered death. You are on the side of
all who have never known love, and who are no longer able to
believe in life. And so you stand against all forms of injustice,
hidden or apparent, and against a growing contempt for man.
In this way, dear brothers and sisters, your whole life needs to
be, like that of John the Baptist, a great, living witness to Jesus
Christ, the Son of God incarnate. Jesus called John "a burning
and shining lamp" (Jn 5:35). You too must be such lamps! Let
your light shine in our society, in political and economic life, in
culture and research. Even if it is only a flicker amid so many
deceptive lights, it nonetheless draws its power and splendor
from the great Morning Star, the Risen Christ, whose light
shines brilliantly—wants to shine brilliantly through us—and
will never fade.

Following Christ—we want to follow him—following
Christ means taking on ever more fully his mind and his way
of life; this is what the Letter to the Philippians tells us: "Let
the same mind be in you that was in Christ!" (cf. Phil 2:5). "To
Look to Christ" is the theme of these days. In looking to him,
the great Teacher of life, the Church has discerned three striking features of Jesus' basic attitude. These three features—with
the Tradition we call them the "evangelical counsels"—have be-

come the distinctive elements of a life committed to the radical following of Christ: poverty, chastity, and obedience. Let us reflect now briefly on them.

Jesus Christ, who was rich with the very richness of God, became poor for our sake, as Saint Paul tells us in the Second Letter to the Corinthians (cf. 2 Cor 8:9); this is an unfathomable statement, one to which we should always return for further reflection. And in the Letter to the Philippians we read, He emptied himself; he humbled himself and became obedient even to death on a Cross (cf. Phil 2:6). The one who himself became poor called the poor "blessed." Saint Luke, in his version of the Beatitudes, makes us understand that this statement—calling the poor blessed—certainly refers to the poor, the truly poor, in Israel at that time, where a sharp distinction existed between rich and poor. But Saint Matthew, in his version of the Beatitudes, explains to us that material poverty alone is not enough to ensure God's closeness, since the heart can be hard and filled with lust for riches. Matthew—like all of Scripture—lets us understand that in any case God is particularly close to the poor. So it becomes evident: in the poor Christians see the Christ who awaits them, who awaits their commitment. Anyone who wants to follow Christ in a radical way must renounce material goods. But he or she must live this poverty in a way centered on Christ, as a means of becoming inwardly free for their neighbor. For all Christians, but especially for us priests, and for religious, both as individuals and in community, the issue of poverty and the poor must be the object of a constant and serious examination of conscience. In our own situation, in which we are not badly off, we are not poor, I think that we ought to reflect particularly on how we can live out this calling in a sincere way. I would like to recommend it for your—for our—examination of conscience.

To understand correctly the meaning of chastity, we must start with its positive content. Once again, we find this only by looking to Christ. Jesus' life had a twofold direction: he lived for the Father and for others. In sacred Scripture we see Jesus as a man of prayer, one who spends entire nights in dialogue with the Father. Through his prayer, he made his own humanity, and the humanity of us all, part of his filial relation to the Father. This dialogue with the Father thus became a constantly renewed mission to the world, to us. Jesus' mission led him to a pure and unreserved commitment to men and women. Sacred Scripture shows that at no moment of his life did he betray even the slightest trace of self-interest or selfishness in his relationship with others. Jesus loved others in the Father, starting from the Father—and thus he loved them in their true being, in their reality. Entering into these sentiments of Jesus Christ—in this total communion with the living God and in this completely pure communion with others, unreservedly at their disposition—this entering into the mind of Christ inspired in Paul a theology and a way of life consonant with Jesus' words about celibacy for the Kingdom of heaven (cf. Mt 19:12). Priests and religious are not aloof from interpersonal relationships. Chastity, on the contrary, means—and this is where I wished to start—an intense relationship; it is, positively speaking, a relationship with the living Christ and, on the basis of that, with the Father. Consequently, by the vow of celibate chastity we do not consecrate ourselves to individualism or a life of isolation; instead, we solemnly promise to put completely and unreservedly at

the service of God's Kingdom—and thus at the service of others—the deep relationships of which we are capable and that
we receive as a gift. In this way priests and religious become
men and women of hope: staking everything on God and thus
showing that God for them is something real, they open up a
space for his presence—the presence of God's Kingdom—in our
world. Dear priests and religious, you have an important contribution to make: amid so much greed, possessiveness, consumerism, and the cult of the individual, we strive to show selfless
love for men and women. We are living lives of hope, a hope
whose fulfillment we leave in God's hands, because we believe
that he will fulfill it. What might have happened had the history
of Christianity lacked such outstanding figures and examples?
What would our world be like, if there were no priests, if there
were no men and women in religious congregations and communities of consecrated life—people whose lives testify to the
hope of a fulfillment beyond every human desire and an experience of the love of God that transcends all human love? Precisely today, the world needs our witness.

We now come to obedience. Jesus lived his entire life, from
the hidden years in Nazareth to the very moment of his death
on the Cross, in listening to the Father, in obedience to the Father. We see this in an exemplary way at Gethsemane. "Not my
will, but yours be done." In this prayer Jesus takes up into his
filial will the stubborn resistance of us all and transforms our
rebelliousness into his obedience. Jesus was a man of prayer. But
at the same time he was also someone who knew how to listen
and to obey: he became "obedient unto death, even death on
a cross" (Phil 2:8). Christians have always known from experi-

ence that, in abandoning themselves to the will of the Father, they lose nothing, but instead discover in this way their deepest identity and interior freedom. In Jesus they have discovered that those who lose themselves find themselves, and those who bind themselves in an obedience grounded in God and inspired by the search for God become free. Listening to God and obeying him has nothing to do with external constraint and the loss of oneself. Only by entering into God's will do we attain our true identity. Our world today needs the testimony of this experience precisely because of its desire for "self-realization" and "self-determination."

Romano Guardini relates in his autobiography how, at a critical moment on his journey, when the faith of his childhood was shaken, the fundamental decision of his entire life—his conversion—came to him through an encounter with the saying of Jesus that only the one who loses himself finds himself (cf. Mk 8:34; Jn 12:25); without self-surrender, without self-loss, there can be no self-discovery or self-realization. But then the question arose: to what extent it is proper to lose myself? To whom can I give myself? It became clear to him that we can surrender ourselves completely only if by doing so we fall into the hands of God. Only in him, in the end, can we lose ourselves and only in him can we find ourselves. But then the question arose: Who is God? Where is God? Then he came to understand that the God to whom we can surrender ourselves is alone the God who became tangible and close to us in Jesus Christ. But once more the question arose: Where do I find Jesus Christ? How can I truly give myself to him? The answer Guardini found after much searching was this: Jesus is concretely present to us only in his

Body, the Church. As a result, obedience to God's will, obedience to Jesus Christ, must be, really and practically, humble obedience to the Church. I think that this too is something calling us to a constant and deep examination of conscience. It is all summed up in the prayer of Saint Ignatius of Loyola—a prayer that always seems to me so overwhelming that I am almost afraid to say it, yet one that, for all its difficulty, we should always repeat: "Take O Lord, and receive all my liberty, my memory, my understanding and my entire will. All that I have and all that I possess you have given me: I surrender it all to you; it is all yours, dispose of it according to your will. Give me only your love and your grace; with these I will be rich enough and will desire nothing more."[8]

Dear brothers and sisters! You are about to return to those places where you live and carry out your ecclesial, pastoral, spiritual, and human activity. May Mary, our great Advocate and Mother, watch over and protect you and your work. May she intercede for you with her Son, our Lord Jesus Christ. I thank you for your prayers and your labors in the Lord's vineyard, and I join you in praying that God will protect and bless all of you, and everyone, particularly the young people, both here in Austria and in the various countries from which many of you have come. With affection I accompany all of you with my blessing.

8. Ignatius of Loyola, *Spiritual Exercises*, trans. Anthony Mottola (New York: Doubleday, 1989), 60.

16. *Set Apart*

From *Homily of His Holiness Benedict XVI, Eucharistic Celebration with Bishops, Seminarians, and Novices*, Apostolic Journey to Sydney on the Occasion of the 23rd World Youth Day, Sydney, Saturday, July 19, 2008

In this noble cathedral I rejoice to greet my brother Bishops and priests, and the deacons, religious, and laity of the Archdiocese of Sydney. In a very special way, my greeting goes to the seminarians and young religious who are present among us. Like the young Israelites in today's first reading, they are a sign of hope and renewal for God's people; and, like those young Israelites, they will have the task of building up the Lord's house in the coming generation. As we admire this magnificent edifice, how can we not think of all those ranks of priests, religious, and faithful laity who, each in his or her own way, contributed to the building up of the Church in Australia? Our thoughts turn in particular to those settler families to whom Father Jeremiah O'Flynn entrusted the Blessed Sacrament at his departure, a "small flock" that cherished and preserved that precious treasure, passing it on to the succeeding generations who raised this great tabernacle to the glory of God. Let us rejoice in their fidelity and perseverance and dedicate ourselves to carrying on their labors for the spread of the Gospel, the conversion of hearts, and the growth of the Church in holiness, unity, and charity!

We are about to celebrate the dedication of the new altar of this venerable cathedral. As its sculpted frontal powerfully reminds us, every altar is a symbol of Jesus Christ, present in the midst of his Church as priest, altar, and victim.[9] Crucified, buried, and raised from the dead, given life in the Spirit, and seated at the right hand of the Father, Christ has become our great high priest, eternally making intercession for us. In the Church's liturgy, and above all in the sacrifice of the Mass consummated on the altars of the world, he invites us, the members of his mystical Body, to share in his self-oblation. He calls us, as the priestly people of the new and eternal covenant, to offer, in union with him, our own daily sacrifices for the salvation of the world.

In today's liturgy the Church reminds us that, like this altar, we too have been consecrated, set apart for the service of God and the building up of his Kingdom. All too often, however, we find ourselves immersed in a world that would set God aside. In the name of human freedom and autonomy, God's name is passed over in silence, religion is reduced to private devotion, and faith is shunned in the public square. At times this mentality, so completely at odds with the core of the Gospel, can even cloud our own understanding of the Church and her mission. We too can be tempted to make the life of faith a matter of mere sentiment, thus blunting its power to inspire a consistent vision of the world and a rigorous dialogue with the many other visions competing for the minds and hearts of our contemporaries.

Yet history, including the history of our own time, shows that the question of God will never be silenced and that indifference to the religious dimension of human existence ultimately diminishes and betrays man himself. Is that not the message

9. Cf. "Preface V of Easter," in *The Roman Missal*, trans. The International Commission on English in the Liturgy, 3rd typical ed., sec. 49 (Washington, D.C.: United States Catholic Conference of Bishops, 2011), 566–67.

that is proclaimed by the magnificent architecture of this cathedral? Is that not the mystery of faith that will be proclaimed from this altar at every celebration of the Eucharist? Faith teaches us that in Jesus Christ, the incarnate Word, we come to understand the grandeur of our own humanity, the mystery of our life on this earth, and the sublime destiny that awaits us in heaven.[10] Faith teaches us that we are God's creatures, made in his image and likeness, endowed with an inviolable dignity, and called to eternal life. Wherever man is diminished, the world around us is also diminished; it loses its ultimate meaning and strays from its goal. What emerges is a culture, not of life, but of death. How could this be considered "progress"? It is a backward step, a form of regression that ultimately dries up the very sources of life for individuals and all of society.

We know that in the end—as St. Ignatius of Loyola saw so clearly—the only real "standard" against which all human reality can be measured is the Cross and its message of an unmerited love that triumphs over evil, sin, and death, creating new life and unfading joy. The Cross reveals that we find ourselves only by giving our lives away, receiving God's love as an unmerited gift, and working to draw all men and women into the beauty of that love and the light of the truth that alone brings salvation to the world.

It is in this truth—this mystery of faith—that we have been "consecrated," (cf. Jn 17:17–19) and it is in this truth that we are called to grow, with the help of God's grace, in daily fidelity to his word, within the life-giving communion of the Church. Yet

10. Second Vatican Council, Pastoral Constitution *Gaudium et Spes* (December 7, 1965), no. 24.

how difficult is this path of consecration! It demands continual "conversion," a sacrificial death to self that is the condition for belonging fully to God, a change of mind and heart that brings true freedom and a new breadth of vision. Today's liturgy offers an eloquent symbol of that progressive spiritual transformation to which each of us is called. From the sprinkling of water, the proclamation of God's word, and the invocation of all the saints, to the prayer of consecration, the anointing and washing of the altar, its being clothed in white and appareled in light—all these rites invite us to relive our own consecration in Baptism. They invite us to reject sin and its false allure and to drink ever more deeply from the life-giving springs of God's grace.

Dear friends, may this celebration, in the presence of the Successor of Peter, be a moment of rededication and renewal for the whole Church in Australia! Here I would like to pause to acknowledge the shame that we have all felt as a result of the sexual abuse of minors by some clergy and religious in this country. Indeed, I am deeply sorry for the pain and suffering the victims have endured, and I assure them that, as their Pastor, I too share in their suffering. These misdeeds, which constitute so grave a betrayal of trust, deserve unequivocal condemnation. They have caused great pain and have damaged the Church's witness. I ask all of you to support and assist your Bishops, and to work together with them in combating this evil. Victims should receive compassion and care, and those responsible for these evils must be brought to justice. It is an urgent priority to promote a safer and more wholesome environment, especially for young people. In these days marked by the celebration of World Youth Day, we are reminded of how precious a treasure has been entrusted to us in our young people and how great a part of the Church's mission in this country has been dedicated to their education and care. As the Church in Australia continues, in the spirit of the Gospel, to address effectively this serious pastoral challenge, I join you in praying that this time of purification will bring about healing, reconciliation, and ever greater fidelity to the moral demands of the Gospel.

I wish now to turn to the seminarians and young religious in our midst, with a special word of affection and encouragement. Dear friends: with great generosity you have set out on a particular path of consecration, grounded in your Baptism and undertaken in response to the Lord's personal call. You have committed yourselves, in different ways, to accepting Christ's invitation to follow him, to leave all behind, and to devote your lives to the pursuit of holiness and the service of his people.

In today's Gospel, the Lord calls us to "believe in the light" (Jn 12:36). These words have a special meaning for you, dear young seminarians and religious. They are a summons to trust in the truth of God's word and to hope firmly in his promises. They invite us to see, with the eyes of faith, the infallible working of his grace all around us, even in those dark times when all our efforts seem to be in vain. Let this altar, with its powerful image of Christ the Suffering Servant, be a constant inspiration to you. Certainly there are times when every faithful disciple will feel the heat and the burden of the day (cf. Mt 20:12) and the struggle of bearing prophetic witness before a world that can appear deaf to the demands of God's word. Do not be afraid! Believe in the light! Take to heart the truth that we have heard in today's second reading: "Jesus Christ is the same, yesterday, today and forever" (Heb 13:8). The light of Easter continues to dispel the darkness!

The Lord also calls us to walk in the light (cf. Jn 12:35). Each of you has embarked on the greatest and the most glorious of all struggles, to be consecrated in truth, to grow in virtue, to achieve harmony between your thoughts and ideals and your words and actions. Enter sincerely and deeply into the discipline and spirit of your programs of formation. Walk in Christ's light daily through fidelity to personal and liturgical prayer, nourished by meditation on the inspired word of God. The Fathers of the Church loved to see the Scriptures as a spiritual Eden, a garden where we can walk freely with God, admiring the beauty and harmony of his saving plan as it bears fruit in our own lives, in the life of the Church, and in all of history. Let prayer, then, and meditation on God's word be the lamp that illumines, purifies, and guides your steps along the path that the Lord has marked out for you. Make the daily celebration of the Eucharist the center of your life. At each Mass, when the Lord's Body and Blood are lifted up at the end of the Eucharistic Prayer, lift up your own hearts and lives, through Christ, with him and in him, in the unity of the Holy Spirit, as a loving sacrifice to God our Father.

In this way, dear young seminarians and religious, you yourselves will become living altars, where Christ's sacrificial love is made present as an inspiration and a source of spiritual nourishment to everyone you meet. By embracing the Lord's call to follow him in chastity, poverty, and obedience, you have begun a journey of radical discipleship that will make you "signs of contradiction" (cf. Lk 2:34) to many of your contemporaries.

Model your lives daily on the Lord's own loving self-oblation in obedience to the will of the Father. You will then discover the freedom and joy that can draw others to the Love that lies beyond all other loves as their source and their ultimate fulfillment. Never forget that celibacy for the sake of the Kingdom means embracing a life completely devoted to love, a love that enables you to commit yourselves fully to God's service and to be totally present to your brothers and sisters, especially those in need. The greatest treasures that you share with other young people—your idealism, your generosity, your time and energy—these are the very sacrifices that you are placing upon the Lord's altar. May you always cherish this beautiful charism that God has given you for his glory and the building up of the Church!

Dear friends, let me conclude these reflections by drawing your attention to the great stained glass window in the chancel of this cathedral. There Our Lady, Queen of Heaven, is represented enthroned in majesty beside her divine Son. The artist has represented Mary, as the new Eve, offering an apple to Christ, the new Adam. This gesture symbolizes her reversal of our first parents' disobedience, the rich fruit that God's grace bore in her own life, and the first fruits of that redeemed and glorified humanity that she has preceded into the glory of heaven. Let us ask Mary, Help of Christians, to sustain the Church in Australia in fidelity to that grace by which the Crucified Lord even now "draws to himself" all creation and every human heart (cf. Jn 12:32). May the power of his Holy Spirit consecrate the faithful of this land in truth and bring forth abundant fruits of holiness and justice for the redemption of the world. May it guide all humanity into the fullness of life around that Altar, where, in the glory of the heavenly liturgy, we are called to sing God's praises forever. Amen.

17. *Instruments of the Holy Spirit*

From *Homily of His Holiness Benedict XVI, Celebration of Vespers with Priests, Religious People, Seminarians, and Deacons,* Apostolic Journey to France, Paris, September 12, 2008

Blessed be God who has brought us together in a place so dear to the heart of every Parisian and all the people of France! Blessed be God, who grants us the grace of offering him our evening prayer and giving him due praise in the very words that the Church's liturgy inherited from the synagogue worship practiced by Christ and his first disciples! Yes, blessed be God for coming to our assistance—*in adiutorium nostrum*—and helping us to offer him our sacrifice of praise!

We are gathered in the Mother Church of the Diocese of Paris, Notre-Dame Cathedral, which rises in the heart of the city as a living sign of God's presence in our midst. My predecessor, Pope Alexander III, laid its first stone, and Popes Pius VII and John Paul II honored it by their presence. I am happy to follow in their footsteps, a quarter of a century after coming here to offer a conference on catechesis. It is hard not to give thanks to the Creator of both matter and spirit for the beauty of this edifice. The Christians of Lutetia had originally built a cathedral dedicated to Saint Stephen, the first martyr; as time went on it became too small and was gradually replaced, between the twelfth and fourteenth centuries, by the great building we admire today. The faith of the Middle Ages built the cathedrals, and here your ancestors came to praise God, to entrust to him their hopes and to express their love for him. Great religious and civil events took place in this shrine, where architects, painters, sculptors, and musicians have given the best of themselves. We need but recall, among so many others, the architect Jean de Chelles, the painter Charles Le Brun, the sculptor Nicolas Coustou, and the organists Louis Vierne and Pierre Cochereau. Art, as a pathway to God, and choral prayer, the Church's praise of the Creator, helped Paul Claudel, who attended Vespers here on Christmas Day 1886, to find the way to a personal experience of God. It is significant that God filled his soul with light during the chanting of the *Magnificat*, in which the Church listens to the song of the Virgin Mary, the Patroness of this church, who reminds the world that the Almighty has lifted up the lowly (cf. Lk 1:52). As the scene of other conversions, less celebrated but no less real, and as the pulpit from which preachers of the Gospel like Fathers Lacordaire, Monsabré, and Samson transmitted the flame of their passion to the most varied congregations, Notre-Dame Cathedral rightly remains one of the most celebrated monuments of your country's heritage. Following a tradition dating back to the time of Saint Louis, I have just venerated the relics of the True Cross and the Crown of Thorns, which have now found a worthy home here, a true offering of the human spirit to the power of creative Love.

Beneath the vaults of this historic Cathedral, which witnesses to the ceaseless dialogue that God wishes to establish with all men and women, his word has just now echoed to become the substance of our evening sacrifice, as expressed in the offering of incense, which makes visible our praise of God. Providentially, the words of the Psalmist describe the emotion filling our souls with an exactness we could hardly have dared to imagine: "I was glad when they said to me, 'Let us go to the house of the Lord!'" (Ps 121:1). *Laetatus sum in his quae dicta sunt mihi*: the Psalmist's joy, brimming over in the very words of the Psalm, penetrates our hearts and resonates deeply within them. We truly rejoice to enter the house of the Lord, since, as the Fathers of the Church have taught us, this house is nothing other than a concrete symbol of Jerusalem on high, which comes down to us (cf. Rv 21:2) to offer us the most beautiful of dwelling places. "If we dwell therein," writes Saint Hilary of Poitiers, "we are fellow citizens of the saints and members of the household of God, for it is the house of God"[11] (*Tract. in Ps.* 121:2). And Saint Augustine adds, "This is a psalm of longing for the heavenly Jerusalem.... It is a Song of Steps, not for going down but for going up.... On our pilgrimage we sigh, in our homeland we will rejoice; but during this exile, we meet companions who have already seen the holy city and urge us to run toward it."[12] Dear friends, during Vespers this evening, we are united in thought and prayer with the voices of the countless men and women who have chanted this psalm in this very place down the centuries. We are united with the pilgrims who went up to Jerusalem and to the steps of its Temple, and with the thousands of men and women who understood that their earthly pilgrimage was to

11. Hilary of Poitiers, *Tractatus Super Psalmos, Patrologia Cursus Completus*, Series Patrologia Latina (PL), edited by Jacques P. Migne (Paris: 1844–64), 9:659.

12. Augustine, *Opera Omnia*, in ibid., 37:1619.

end in heaven, in the eternal Jerusalem, trusting Christ to guide them there. What joy indeed, to know that we are invisibly surrounded by so great a crowd of witnesses!

Our pilgrimage to the holy city would not be possible if it were not made in the Church, the seed and the prefiguration of the heavenly Jerusalem. "Unless the Lord builds the house, those who build it labor in vain" (Ps 126:1). Who is this Lord, if not our Lord Jesus Christ? It is he who founded his Church and built it on rock, on the faith of the Apostle Peter. In the words of Saint Augustine, "It is Jesus Christ our Lord who himself builds his temple. Many indeed labor to build, yet unless the Lord intervenes to build, in vain do the builders labor."[13] Dear friends, Augustine goes on to ask how we can know who these builders are, and his answer is this: "All those who preach God's word in the Church, all who are ministers of God's divine Sacraments. All of us run, all of us work, all of us build," yet it is God alone who, within us, "builds, exhorts, and inspires awe; who opens our understanding and guides our minds to faith."[14] What marvels surround our work in the service of God's word! We are instruments of the Holy Spirit; God is so humble that he uses us to spread his word. We become his voice, once we have listened carefully to the word coming from his mouth. We place his word on our lips in order to bring it to the world. He accepts the offering of our prayer, and through it he communicates himself to everyone we meet. Truly, as Paul tells the Ephesians, "he has blessed us in Christ with every spiritual blessing" (Eph 1:3), for he has chosen us to be his witnesses to the ends of the earth, and

13. Ibid., 37:1670.
14. Ibid.

he made us his elect, even before we came into existence, by a mysterious gift of his grace.

God's Word, the Eternal Word, who was with him from the beginning (cf. Jn 1:1), was born of a woman, born a subject of the law, in order to redeem the subjects of the law, "to redeem those who were under the law, so that we might receive adoption as sons" (cf. Gal 4:4–5). The Son of God took flesh in the womb of a woman, a virgin. Your cathedral is a living hymn of stone and light in praise of that act, unique in the annals of human history: the eternal Word of God entering our history in the fullness of time to redeem us by his self-offering in the sacrifice of the Cross. Our earthly liturgies, entirely ordered to the celebration of this unique act within history, will never fully express its infinite meaning. Certainly, the beauty of our celebrations can never be sufficiently cultivated, fostered, and refined, for nothing can be too beautiful for God, who is himself infinite Beauty. Yet our earthly liturgies will never be more than a pale reflection of the liturgy celebrated in the Jerusalem on high, the goal of our pilgrimage on earth. May our own celebrations nonetheless resemble that liturgy as closely as possible and grant us a foretaste of it!

Even now the word of God is given to us as the soul of our apostolate, the soul of our priestly life. Each morning the word awakens us. Each morning the Lord himself "opens our ear" (cf. Is 50:5) through the psalms in the Office of Readings and Morning Prayer. Throughout the day, the word of God becomes the substance of the prayer of the whole Church, as she bears witness in this way to her fidelity to Christ. In the celebrated phrase of Saint Jerome, to be taken up in the 12th Assembly of the Synod of Bishops next month, "Ignorance of the Scriptures is ignorance of Christ."[15] Dear brother priests, do not be afraid to spend much time reading and meditating on the Scriptures and praying the Divine Office! Almost without your knowing it, God's word, read and pondered in the Church, acts upon you and transforms you. As the manifestation of divine Wisdom, if that word becomes your life "companion," it will be your "good counselor" and an "encouragement in cares and grief" (Ws 8:9).

"The word of God is living and active, sharper than any two-edged sword," as the author of the Letter to the Hebrews tells us (Heb 4:12). Dear seminarians, who are preparing to receive the sacrament of Holy Orders and thus to share in the threefold office of teaching, governing, and sanctifying, this word is given to you as a precious treasure. By meditating on it daily, you will enter into the very life of Christ that you will be called to radiate all around you. By his word, the Lord Jesus instituted the Holy Sacrament of his Body and Blood; by his word, he healed the sick, cast out demons, and forgave sins; by his word, he revealed to us the hidden mysteries of his Kingdom. You are called to become stewards of this word that accomplishes what it communicates. Always cultivate a thirst for the word of God! Thus you will learn to love everyone you meet along life's journey. In the Church everyone has a place, everyone! Every person can and must find a place in her.

And you, dear deacons, effective coworkers of the Bishops and priests, continue to love the word of God! You proclaim the Gospel at the heart of the Eucharistic celebration, and you

15. Jerome, *Commentarium in Isaiam Prophetam Libri XVIII prol.*, *Patrologia Cursus Completus*, PL., 24, 17B:31.

expound it in the catechesis you offer to your brothers and sisters. Make the Gospel the center of your lives, of your service to your neighbors, of your entire *diakonia*. Without seeking to take the place of priests, but assisting them with your friendship and your activity, may you be living witnesses to the infinite power of God's word!

In a particular way, men and women religious and all consecrated persons draw life from the Wisdom of God expressed in his word. The profession of the evangelical counsels has configured you, dear consecrated persons, to Christ, who for our sakes became poor, obedient, and chaste. Your only treasure— which, to tell the truth, will alone survive the passage of time and the curtain of death—is the word of the Lord. It is he who said, "Heaven and earth will pass away; my words will not pass away" (Mt 24:35). Your obedience is, etymologically, a "hearing," for the word "obey" comes from the Latin *"obaudire,"* meaning to turn one's ear to someone or something. In obeying, you turn your soul toward the one who is the Way, and the Truth, and the Life (cf. Jn 14:6), and who says to you, as Saint Benedict taught his monks, "Listen carefully, my son, to the Master's instructions, and attend to them with the ear of your heart."[16] Finally, let yourselves be purified daily by him who said, "Every branch that bears fruit my Father prunes, to make it bear more fruit" (Jn 15:2). The purity of God's word is the model for your own chastity, ensuring its spiritual fruitfulness.

With unfailing confidence in the power of God, who has saved us "in hope" (cf. Rom 8:24) and who wishes to make of

16. St. Benedict, *The Rule of Saint Benedict*, trans. Timothy Fry (New York: Vintage), 3.

us one flock under the guidance of one shepherd, Christ Jesus, I pray for the unity of the Church. I greet once again with respect and affection the representatives of the Christian Churches and ecclesial communities who, as our brothers and sisters, have come to pray Vespers together with us in this cathedral. So great is the power of God's word that we can all be entrusted to it, remembering what Saint Paul once did, our privileged intercessor during this year. As Paul took leave of the presbyters of Ephesus at Miletus, he did not hesitate to entrust them "to God and to the word of his grace" (Acts 20:32), while warning them against every form of division. I implore the Lord to increase within us the sense of this unity of the word of God, which is the sign, pledge, and guarantee of the unity of the Church: there is no love in the Church without love of the word, no Church without unity around Christ the Redeemer, no fruits of redemption without love of God and neighbor, according to the two commandments that sum up all of Sacred Scripture!

Dear brothers and sisters, in Our Lady we have the finest example of fidelity to God's word. Her great fidelity found fulfillment in the Incarnation; with absolute confidence, Mary can say, "Behold the handmaid of the Lord; let it be done to me according to your word!" (Lk 1:38). Our evening prayer is about to take up the *Magnificat*, the song of her whom all generations will call blessed. Mary believed in the fulfillment of the words the Lord had spoken to her (cf. Lk 1:45); she hoped against all hope in the resurrection of her Son; and so great was her love for humanity that she was given to us as our Mother (cf. Jn 19:27). Thus we see that "Mary is completely at home with the word of God; with ease she moves in and out of it. She speaks and thinks with the word of God; the word of God becomes her word, and her word issues from the word of God."[17] To her, then, we can say with confidence, "Holy Mary, Mother of God, our Mother, teach us to believe, to hope, to love with you. Show us the way to his Kingdom!"[18] Amen.

18. *Inflamed with His Hope*

From *Homily of His Holiness Benedict XVI*, Celebration of Vespers with Priests, Men and Women Religious, Seminarians, and Ecclesial Movements, Amman, May 9, 2009

To all of you and to the priests, Sisters and Brothers, seminarians, and lay faithful gathered here this evening I express my sincere thanks for giving me this opportunity to pray with you and to experience something of the richness of our liturgical traditions.

The Church herself is a pilgrim people and thus, through the centuries, has been marked by determinant historical events and pervading cultural epochs. Sadly, some of these have included times of theological dispute or periods of repression. Others, however, have been moments of reconciliation—marvelously strengthening the communion of the Church—and times of rich cultural revival, to which Eastern Christians have contributed so greatly. Particular Churches within the universal Church attest to the dynamism of her earthly journey and manifest to all members of the faithful a treasure of spiritual, liturgical, and ec-

17. Cf. Pope Benedict XVI, Encyclical Letter *Deus Caritas Est*, no. 41.
18. Cf. Pope Benedict XVI, Encyclical Letter *Spe Salvi*, no. 50.

clesiastical traditions that point to God's universal goodness and his will, seen throughout history, to draw all into his divine life.

The ancient living treasure of the traditions of the Eastern Churches enriches the universal Church and could never be understood simply as objects to be passively preserved. All Christians are called to respond actively to the Lord's mandate—as Saint George did in dramatic ways according to popular record—to bring others to know and love him. In fact the vicissitudes of history have strengthened the members of particular Churches to embrace this task with vigor and to engage resolutely with the pastoral realities of today. Most of you trace ancient links to the Patriarchate of Antioch, and your communities are thus rooted here in the Near East. And, just as two thousand years ago it was in Antioch that the disciples were first called Christians, so also today, as small minorities in scattered communities across these lands, you too are recognized as followers of the Lord. The public face of your Christian faith is certainly not restricted to the spiritual solicitude you bear for one another and your people, essential though that is. Rather, your many works of universal charity extend to all Jordanians—Muslims and those of other religions—and also to the large numbers of refugees whom this Kingdom so generously welcomes.

Dear brothers and sisters, the first Psalm (cf. Ps 103) we prayed this evening presents us with glorious images of God the bountiful Creator, actively present in his creation, providing life with abundant goodness and wise order, ever ready to renew the face of the earth! The Epistle reading we have just heard, however, paints a different picture. It warns us, not in a threatening way, but realistically, of the need to stay alert, to be aware of the forces of evil at work creating darkness in our world (cf. Eph 6:10–20). Some might be tempted to think this a contradiction; yet reflecting on our ordinary human experience we recognize spiritual struggle, we acknowledge the daily need to move into Christ's light, to choose life, to seek truth. Indeed, this rhythm—turning away from evil and girding ourselves with the Lord's strength—is what we celebrate at every Baptism, the gateway to Christian life, the first step along the way of the Lord's disciples. Recalling Christ's baptism by John in the waters of the Jordan, the assembled pray that the one to be baptized will be rescued from the kingdom of darkness and brought into the splendor of God's kingdom of light, and so receive the gift of new life.

This dynamic movement from death to newness of life, from darkness to light, from despair to hope, that we experience so dramatically during the Triduum, and is celebrated with great joy in the season of Easter, ensures that the Church herself remains young. She is alive because Christ is alive, truly risen. Vivified by the presence of the Spirit, she reaches out every day, drawing men and women to the living Lord. Dear Bishops, priests, Brothers and Sisters, dear lay faithful, our respective roles of service and mission within the Church are the tireless response of a pilgrim people. Your liturgies, ecclesiastical discipline, and spiritual heritage are a living witness to your unfolding tradition. You amplify the echo of the first Gospel proclamation, you render fresh the ancient memories of the works of the Lord, you make present his saving graces, and you diffuse anew the first glimmers of the Easter light and the flickering flames of Pentecost.

In this way, imitating Christ and the Old Testament patriarchs and prophets, we set out to lead people from the desert toward the place of life, toward the Lord who gives us life in abundance. This marks all your apostolic works, the variety and caliber of which are greatly appreciated. From kindergartens to places of higher education, from orphanages to homes for the elderly, from work with refugees to a music academy, medical clinics and hospitals, interreligious dialogue and cultural initiatives, your presence in this society is a marvelous sign of the hope that defines us as Christian.

That hope reaches far beyond the confines of our own Christian communities. So often you find that the families of other religions, with whom you work and offer your service of universal charity, hold concerns and worries that cross religious and cultural boundaries. This is especially noticeable in regard to the hopes and aspirations of parents for their children. What parent or person of good will could not be troubled by the negative influences so pervasive in our globalized world, including the destructive elements within the entertainment industry that so callously exploit the innocence and sensibility of the vulnerable and the young? Yet, with your eyes firmly fixed on Christ, the light who dispels all evil, restores lost innocence, and humbles earthly pride, you will sustain a magnificent vision of hope for all those you meet and serve.

May I conclude with a special word of encouragement to those present who are in formation for the priesthood and religious life. Guided by the light of the Risen Lord, inflamed with his hope, and vested with his truth and love, your witness will bring abundant blessings to those whom you meet along the way. Indeed the same holds for all young Christian Jordanians: do not be afraid to make your own wise, measured, and respectful contribution to the public life of the Kingdom. The authentic voice of faith will always bring integrity, justice, compassion, and peace!

Dear friends, with sentiments of great respect for all of you gathered with me this evening in worship, I again thank you for your prayers for my ministry as the Successor of Peter, and I assure you and all those entrusted to your pastoral care of a remembrance in my own daily prayer.

19. *Abide in My Love*

From *Lectio Divina of His Holiness Benedict XVI*, Pontifical
Roman Major Seminary, Rome, February 12, 2010

Every year it is a great joy to me to be with the seminarians of the Diocese of Rome, young men who are preparing themselves to respond to the Lord's call to be laborers in his vineyard and priests of his mystery. This is the joy of seeing that the Church lives, that the Church's future is also present in our region and, precisely, also in Rome.

In this Year for Priests let us be particularly attentive to the Lord's words about our service. The Gospel Passage that has just been read speaks indirectly but profoundly of our sacrament, of our call to be in the Lord's vineyard, to be servants of his mystery.

In this brief passage (cf. Jn 15:1-17) we find certain key words that give an idea of the proclamation that the Lord wishes to make with this text. "Abide": in this short passage we find the word "abide" ten times. We then find the new commandment:

"Love one another as I have loved you" (Jn 15:12); "No longer do I call you servants ... but friends" (Jn 15:15); "bear fruit" (Jn 15:8); and lastly, "Ask, and it will be given you ... that your joy may be full" (Jn 15:7). Let us pray to the Lord that he may help us enter into the meaning of his words, that these words may penetrate our hearts, thus becoming in us the way and life, with us and through us.

The first words are, "Abide in me ... in my love" (cf. Jn 15:9). Abiding in the Lord is fundamental as the first topic of this passage. Abide: where? In love, in the love of Christ, in being loved and in loving the Lord. The whole of chapter 15 explains where we are to abide, because the first eight verses explain and present the Parable of the Vine: "I am the vine, you are the branches" (Jn 15:5). The vine is an Old Testament image that we find in both the Prophets and the Psalms, and it has a double meaning: it is a parable for the People of God that is his vineyard. He planted a vine in this world, he tended this vine, he tended his vineyard, he protected his vineyard, and what was his intention? It was of course to produce fruit, to harvest the precious gift of grapes, of good wine.

And thus the second meaning appears: wine is a symbol, the expression of the joy of love. The Lord created his people to find the answer to his love. This image of the vine, of the vineyard, thus has a spousal meaning, it is an expression of the fact that God seeks his creature's love, through his Chosen People he wants to enter into a relationship of love, a spousal relationship with the world.

Then, however, history proved to be a history of infidelity: instead of precious grapes, only small "inedible fruits" are produced. The response of this great love is not forthcoming, this unity, this unconditional union between man and God in the communion of love does not come about, man withdraws into himself, he wants to keep himself to himself, he wants to have God for himself, he wants the world for himself. Consequently the vineyard is devastated, the boar from the forest and all the enemies arrive, and the vineyard becomes a wilderness.

But God does not give up. God finds a new way of reaching a free, irrevocable love, the fruit of this love, the true grape: God becomes man, and thus he himself becomes the root of the vine, he himself becomes the vine, and so the vine becomes indestructible. This people of God cannot be destroyed for God himself has entered it, he has put down roots in this land. The new People of God are truly founded in God himself who becomes man and thus calls us to be the new vine in him and to abide in him, to dwell in him.

Let us also bear in mind that in chapter 6 of John's Gospel we find the Discourse of the Bread that becomes the great Discourse on the Eucharistic mystery. In this chapter 15 we have the Discourse on the Vine: the Lord does not speak explicitly of the Eucharist. Naturally, however, behind the mystery of the wine is the reality that he has made himself fruit and wine for us, that his Blood is the fruit of the love born from the earth forever and, in the Eucharist, this Blood becomes our blood, we are renewed, we receive a new identity because Christ's Blood becomes our blood. Thus we are related to God in the Son and, in the Eucharist, this great reality of life in which we are branches joined to the Son and thereby in union with eternal love becomes our reality.

"Abide": abide in this great mystery, abide in this new gift of the Lord that has made us a people in itself, in his Body and with his Blood. It seems to me that we must meditate deeply on this mystery, that is, that God makes himself Body, one with us; Blood, one with us; that we may abide in this mystery in communion with God himself, in this great history of love that is the history of true happiness. In meditating on this gift—God made himself one of us, and at the same time he made us all one, a single vine—we must also begin to pray so that this mystery may penetrate our minds and hearts ever more deeply and that we may be ever more capable of living the greatness of the mystery and thus to begin experiencing the commandment to abide in our lives.

If we continue to read this Gospel passage attentively, we also find a second imperative: "observe my commandments" (cf. Jn 15:10). "Observe" only comes second. "Abide" comes first at the ontological level, namely that we are united with him, he has given himself to us beforehand and has already given us his love, the fruit. It is not we who must produce the abundant fruit; Christianity is not moralism, it is not we who must do all that God expects of the world, but we must first of all enter this ontological mystery: God gives himself. His being, his loving, precedes our action and, in the context of his Body, in the context of being in him, being identified with him and ennobled with his Blood, we too can act with Christ.

Ethics are a consequence of being: first the Lord gives us new life; this is the great gift. Being precedes action, and from this being action then follows, as an organic reality, for we can also be what we are in our activity. Let us thus thank the Lord, for he has removed us from pure moralism; we cannot obey a prescribed law but must only act in accordance with our new identity. Therefore it is no longer obedience, an external thing, but rather the fulfillment of the gift of new life.

I say it once again: let us thank the Lord because he goes before us, he gives us what we must give, and we must then be, in the truth and by virtue of our new being, protagonists of his reality. Abiding and observing: observing is the sign of abiding and abiding is the gift that he gives us but that must be renewed every day of our lives.

Next comes this new commandment: "love one another as I have loved you" (Jn 15:12). There is no greater love than this, "that a man lay down his life for his friends" (Jn 15:13). What does this mean? Here too it is not a question of moralism. Some might say, "It is not a new commandment; the commandment to love one's neighbor as oneself already exists in the Old Testament." Others say, "This love should be even more radicalized; this love of others must imitate Christ who gave himself for us; it must be a heroic love, to the point of the gift of self." In this case, however, Christianity would be a heroic moralism. It is true that we must reach the point of this radicalism of love that Christ showed to us and gave for us, but here too the true newness is not what we do, the true newness is what he did: the Lord gave us himself, and the Lord gave us the true newness of being members of his Body, of being branches of the vine that he is. Therefore, the newness is the gift, the great gift, and from the gift, from the newness of the gift, also follows, as I have said, the new action.

St. Thomas Aquinas says this very succinctly when he writes,

"The New Law is the grace of the Holy Spirit."[19] The New Law is not another commandment more difficult than the others: the New Law is a gift, the New Law is the presence of the Holy Spirit imparted to us in the sacrament of Baptism, in Confirmation, and given to us every day in the Most Blessed Eucharist. The Fathers distinguished here between *"sacramentum"* and *"exemplum."* *"Sacramentum"* is the gift of the new being, and this gift also becomes an example for our action, but *"sacramentum"* precedes it, and we live by the sacrament. Here we see the centrality of the sacrament that is the centrality of the gift.

Let us proceed in our reflection. The Lord says, "No longer do I call you servants, for the servant does not know what his master is doing; but I have called you friends, for all that I have heard from my Father I have made known to you" (Jn 15:15). No longer servants who obey orders, but friends who know, who are united in the same will, in the same love. Hence the newness is that God has made himself known, that God has shown himself that God is no longer the unknown God, sought but not found or only perceived from afar. God has shown himself: in the Face of Christ we see God, God has made himself "known," and has thereby made us his friends. Let us think how, in humanity's history, in all the archaic religions, it is known that there is a God. This knowledge is deeply rooted in the human heart, the knowledge that God is one, that deities are not "the" God. Yet this God remains very distant, he does not seem to make himself known, he does not make himself loved, he is not a friend, but is remote. Religions, therefore, were not very

19. St. Thomas Aquinas, *Summa Theologiae* I-II, q. 106, a. 1.

concerned with this God, concrete life was concerned with the spirits that we meet every day and with which we must reckon daily. God remained distant.

Then we see the great philosophical movement: let us think of Plato and Aristotle who began to understand that this God is the *agathon*, goodness itself, that he is the *eros* that moves the world; yet this remains a human thought, it is an idea of God that comes close to the truth, but it is an idea of ours, and God remains the hidden God.

A Regensburg professor recently wrote to me, a professor of physics who had read my Discourse to the University very late. He wrote to tell me that he could not agree, or not fully, with my logic. He said, "Of course, the idea is convincing that the rational structure of the world demands a creative reason that made this rationality which is not explained by itself." And he continued, "But if a demiurge can exist," this is how he put it, "a demiurge seems to me certain by what you say, I do not see that there is a God who is good, just, and merciful. I can see that there is a reason that precedes the rationality of the cosmos, but I cannot see the rest." Thus God remains hidden to him. It is a reason that precedes our reasoning, our rationality, the rationality of being, but eternal love does not exist, the great mercy that gives us life does not exist.

And here, in Christ, God showed himself in his total truth, he showed that he is reason and love, that eternal reason is love and thus creates. Unfortunately, today too, many people live far from Christ, they do not know his face and thus the eternal temptation of dualism, which is also hidden in this professor's letter, is constantly renewed, in other words perhaps there is not only one good principle but also a bad principle, a principle of evil; perhaps the world is divided and there are two equally strong realities and the Good God is only part of the reality. Today, even in theology, including Catholic theology, this thesis is being disseminated: that God is not almighty. Thus an apology is sought for God who would not, therefore, be responsible for the great store of evil we encounter in the world. But what a feeble apology! A God who is not almighty! Evil is not in his hands! And how could we possibly entrust ourselves to this God? How could we be certain of his love if this love ended where the power of evil began?

However, God is no longer unknown: in the Face of the Crucified Christ we see God and we see true omnipotence, not the myth of omnipotence. For us human beings, almightiness, power, is always identified with the capacity to destroy, to do evil. Nevertheless the true concept of omnipotence that appears in Christ is precisely the opposite: in him true omnipotence is loving to the point that God can suffer: here his true omnipotence is revealed, which can even go as far as a love that suffers for us. And thus we see that he is the true God and the true God, who is love, is power: the power of love. And we can trust ourselves to his almighty love and live in this, with this almighty love.

I think we should always meditate anew on this reality, that we should thank God because he has shown himself, because we know his Face, we know him face to face; no longer like Moses who could only see the back of the Lord. This too is a beautiful idea of which St. Gregory of Nyssa said, "Seeing only his back, means that we must always follow Christ."[20] But at the same

20. Cf. St. Gregory of Nyssa, *The Life of Moses*, trans. Abraham J. Malherbe and Everett Ferguson (New York: Paulist Press, 1978).

time God showed us his Countenance with Christ, his Face. The curtain of the temple was torn. It opened, the mystery of God is visible. The first commandment that excludes images of God because they might only diminish his reality is changed, renewed, taking another form. Today we can see God's Face in Christ the man, we can have an image of Christ and thus see who God is.

I think that those who have understood this, who have been touched by this mystery, that God has revealed himself, that the curtain of the temple has been torn asunder, that he has shown his Face, find a source of permanent joy. We can only say, "Thank you. Yes, now we know who you are, who God is, and how to respond to him." And I think that this joy of knowing God who has shown himself, to the depths of his being, also embraces the joy of communicating this: those who have understood this, who live touched by this reality, must do as the first disciples did when they went to their friends and brethren saying, "We have found the one of whom the Prophets spoke. He is present now" (Jn 1:45). Mission is not an external appendix to the faith but rather the dynamism of faith itself. Those who have seen, who have encountered Jesus, must go to their friends and tell them, "We have found him, he is Jesus, the One who was Crucified for us."

Then, continuing, the text says, "I chose you and appointed you that you should go and bear fruit and that your fruit should abide" (Jn 15:16). With this we return to the beginning, to the image, to the Parable of the Vine: it is created to bear fruit. And what is the fruit? As we have said, the fruit is love. In the Old Testament, with the Torah as the first stage of God's revelation of himself, the fruit was understood as justice, that is, living in accordance with the Word of God, living in accordance with God's will, hence, living well.

This continues but at the same time is transcended: true justice does not consist in obedience to a few norms, rather it is love, creative love that finds in itself the riches and abundance of good. Abundance is one of the key words of the New Testament. God himself always gives in abundance. In order to create man, he creates this abundance of an immense cosmos; to redeem man he gives himself, in the Eucharist he gives himself. And anyone who is united with Christ, who is a branch of the Vine and who abides by this law does not ask, "Can I still do this or not?" "Should I do this or not?" Rather, he lives in the enthusiasm of love that does not ask, "Is this still necessary or is it forbidden?" but simply, in the creativity of love, wants to live with Christ and for Christ and give his whole self to him, thus entering into the joy of bearing fruit. Let us also bear in mind that the Lord says, "I chose you and appointed you that you should go" (Jn 15:16). This is the dynamism that dwells in Christ's love; to go, in other words, not to remain alone for me, to see my perfection, to guarantee eternal beatification for me, but rather to forget myself, to go as Christ went, to go as God went from the immensity of his majesty to our poverty, to find fruit, to help us, to give us the possibility of bearing the true fruit of love. The fuller we are of this joy in having discovered God's Face, the more real will the enthusiasm of love in us be, and it will bear fruit.

And finally, we come to the last words in this passage: "Whatever you ask the Father in my name, he may give it to you" (Jn 15:16): a brief catechesis on prayer that never ceases to surprise us. Twice in this chapter 15 the Lord says, "ask whatever you will, and it shall be done for you" (Jn 15:7, 16), and he says it once more in chapter 16. And we want to say, "But no, Lord it is not true." There are so many good and deeply felt prayers of mothers who pray for a dying child that are not heard, so many prayers that something good will happen and the Lord does not grant it. What does this promise mean? In chapter 16 the Lord offers us the key to understanding it: he tells us what he gives us, what all this is, *chara*, joy. If someone has found joy he has found all things and sees all things in the light of divine love. Like St. Francis, who wrote the great poem on creation in a bleak situation, yet even there, close to the suffering Lord, he rediscovered the beauty of being, the goodness of God, and composed this great poem.

It is also useful to remember at the same time some verses of Luke's Gospel, in which the Lord, in a parable, speaks of prayer, saying, "If you then, who are evil, know how to give good gifts to your children, how much more will the heavenly Father give the Holy Spirit to those who ask him?" (Lk 11:13). The Holy Spirit, in the Gospel according to Luke, is joy, in John's Gospel he is the same reality: joy is the Holy Spirit, and the Holy Spirit is joy, or, in other words from God, we do not ask something small or great, from God we invoke the divine gift, God himself; this is the great gift that God gives us: God himself. In this regard we must learn to pray, to pray for the great reality, for the divine reality, so that God may give us himself, may give us his Spirit, and thus we may respond to the demands of life and help others in their suffering. Of course, he teaches us the "Our Father." We can pray for many things. In all our needs we can pray, "Help me!" This is very human, and God is human, as we have seen; therefore it is right to pray God also for the small things of our daily lives.

However, at the same time, prayer is a journey, I would say [a] flight of stairs: we must learn more and more what it is that we can pray for and what we cannot pray for because it is an expression of our selfishness. I cannot pray for things that are harmful for others, I cannot pray for things that help my egoism, my pride. Thus prayer, in God's eyes, becomes a process of purification of our thoughts, of our desires. As the Lord says in the Parable of the Vine, we must be pruned, purified, every day; living with Christ, in Christ, abiding in Christ, is a process of purification, and it is only in this process of slow purification, of liberation from ourselves and from the desire to have only ourselves, that the true journey of life lies and the path of joy unfolds.

As I have already said, all the Lord's words have a sacramental background. The fundamental background for the Parable of the Vine is Baptism: we are implanted in Christ; and the Eucharist: we are one loaf, one body, one blood, one life with Christ. Thus this process of purification also has a sacramental background: the sacrament of Penance, of Reconciliation, in which we accept this divine pedagogy that day by day, throughout our life, purifies us and increasingly makes us true members of his Body. In this way we can learn that God responds to our prayers, that he often responds with his goodness also to small prayers, but often too he corrects them, transforms them, and guides them so that we may at last and really be branches of his Son, of the true vine, members of his Body.

Let us thank God for the greatness of his love, let us pray that he may help us to grow in his love and truly to abide in his love.

20. *Fix Your Eyes upon Him*

From *Homily of His Holiness Benedict XVI, Eucharist with Seminarians,* Apostolic Journey to Madrid on the Occasion of the 26th World Youth Day, Madrid, August 20, 2011

I am very pleased to celebrate Holy Mass with you who aspire to be Christ's priests for the service of the Church and of man, and I thank you for the kind words with which you welcomed me. Today, this holy cathedral church of Santa María La Real de la Almudena is like a great Upper Room, where the Lord greatly desires to celebrate the Passover with you who wish one day to preside in his name at the mysteries of salvation. Looking at you, I again see proof of how Christ continues to call young disciples and to make them his apostles, thus keeping alive the mission of the Church and the offer of the Gospel to the world. As seminarians you are on the path toward a sacred goal: to continue the mission that Christ received from the Father. Called by him, you have followed his voice and, attracted by his loving gaze, you now advance toward the sacred ministry. Fix your eyes upon him who through his incarnation is the supreme revelation of God to the world and who through his resurrection faithfully fulfills his promise. Give thanks to him for this sign of favor in which he holds each one of you.

The first reading that we heard shows us Christ as the new and eternal priest who made of himself a perfect offering. The response to the psalm may be aptly applied to him since, at his coming into the world, he said to the Father, "Here I am to do your will" (cf. Ps 39:8). He tried to please him in all things: in his words and actions, along the way or welcoming sinners. His life was one of service, and his longing was a constant prayer, placing himself in the name of all before the Father as the first-born son of many brothers and sisters. The author of the Letter to the Hebrews states that, by a single offering, he brought to perfection for all time those of us who are called to share his Sonship (cf. Heb 10:14).

The Eucharist, whose institution is mentioned in the Gospel just proclaimed (cf. Lk 22:14–20), is the real expression of that unconditional offering of Jesus for all, even for those who betrayed him. It was the offering of his body and blood for the life of mankind and for the forgiveness of sins. His blood, a sign of life, was given to us by God as a covenant, so that we might apply the force of his life wherever death reigns due to our sins, and thus destroy it. Christ's body broken and his blood outpoured—the surrender of his freedom—became through these Eucharistic signs the new source of mankind's redeemed freedom. In Christ, we have the promise of definitive redemption and the certain hope of future blessings. Through Christ we know that we are not walking toward the abyss, the silence of nothingness or death, but are rather pilgrims on the way to a promised land, on the way to him who is our end and our beginning.

Dear friends, you are preparing yourselves to become apostles with Christ and like Christ, and to accompany your fellow men and women along their journey as companions and servants.

How should you behave during these years of preparation? First of all, they should be years of interior silence, of unceasing prayer, of constant study, and of gradual insertion into the pastoral activity and structures of the Church. A Church that is community and institution, family and mission, the creation of Christ through his Holy Spirit, as well as the result of those of us who shape it through our holiness and our sins. God, who does not hesitate to make of the poor and of sinners his friends and instruments for the redemption of the human race, willed it so. The holiness of the Church is above all the objective holiness of the very person of Christ, of his Gospel and his sacraments, the holiness of that power from on high that enlivens and impels it. We have to be saints so as not to create a contradiction between the sign that we are and the reality that we wish to signify.

Meditate well upon this mystery of the Church, living the years of your formation in deep joy, humbly, clear-mindedly, and with radical fidelity to the Gospel, in an affectionate relation to the time spent and the people among whom you live. No one chooses the place or the people to whom he is sent, and every time has its own challenges; but in every age God gives the right grace to face and overcome those challenges with love and realism. That is why, no matter the circumstances in which he finds and however difficult they may be, the priest must grow in all kinds of good works, keeping alive within him the words spoken on his Ordination day, by which he was exhorted to model his life on the mystery of the Lord's cross.

To be modeled on Christ, dear seminarians, is to be identified ever more closely with him who, for our sake, became servant, priest, and victim. To be modeled on him is in fact the task upon which the priest spends his entire life. We already know that it is beyond us and we will not fully succeed, but, as St. Paul says, we run toward the goal, hoping to reach it (cf. Phil 3:12–14).

That said, Christ the High Priest is also the Good Shepherd who cares for his sheep, even giving his life for them (cf. Jn 10:11). In order to liken yourselves to the Lord in this as well, your heart must mature while in seminary, remaining completely open to the Master. This openness, which is a gift of the Holy Spirit, inspires the decision to live in celibacy for the sake of the kingdom of heaven and, leaving aside the world's goods, live in austerity of life and sincere obedience, without pretense.

Ask him to let you imitate him in his perfect charity toward all, so that you do not shun the excluded and sinners, but help them convert and return to the right path. Ask him to teach you how to be close to the sick and the poor in simplicity and generosity. Face this challenge without anxiety or mediocrity, but rather as a beautiful way of living our human life in gratuitousness and service, as witnesses of God made man, messengers of the supreme dignity of the human person and therefore its unconditional defenders. Relying on his love, do not be intimidated by surroundings that would exclude God and in which power, wealth, and pleasure are frequently the main criteria ruling people's lives. You may be shunned along with others who propose higher goals or who unmask the false gods before whom many now bow down. That will be the moment when a life deeply rooted in Christ will clearly be seen as something new, and it will powerfully attract those who truly search for God, truth, and justice.

Under the guidance of your formators, open your hearts to

the light of the Lord, to see if this path that demands courage and authenticity is for you. Approach the priesthood only if you are firmly convinced that God is calling you to be his ministers and if you are completely determined to exercise it in obedience to the Church's precepts.

With this confidence, learn from him who described himself as meek and humble of heart, leaving behind all earthly desire for his sake so that, rather than pursuing your own good, you build up your brothers and sisters by the way you live, as did the patron saint of the diocesan clergy of Spain, St. John of Avila. Moved by his example, look above all to the Virgin Mary, Mother of Priests. She will know how to mold your hearts according to the model of Christ, her divine Son, and she will teach you how to treasure forever all that he gained on Calvary for the salvation of the world. Amen.

21. Do Not Be Conformed to This World

From *Lectio Divina of His Holiness Benedict XVI*, Pontifical
Roman Seminary, February 15, 2012

On the day of Our Lady of Trust, it gives me great joy to see my seminarians, the seminarians of Rome, on their way toward the priesthood and thus to see the Church of the future, the Church that is ever alive.

Today we have heard a text—we hear it and we meditate upon it—from the Letter to the Romans: Paul speaks to the Romans and therefore speaks to us, because he is speaking to Romans of all the epochs. This Letter is not only St. Paul's greatest, but it is also extraordinary because of its doctrinal and spiritual weight. And it is extraordinary because it is a letter written to a community he had neither founded nor even visited. He writes to announce his visit and express his desire to visit Rome, and he announces in advance the essential content of his *kerygma*; in this way he prepares the City for his visit. He writes to this community, with which he is not personally acquainted, because he is the Apostle to the Gentiles—of the transmission of the Gospel of the Jews to the Gentiles—and Rome is the capital of the Gentiles and hence the center, and the destination of his message, too.

The Gospel had to arrive here, so that it might really reach the pagan world. It was to arrive, but in a different way from that which he had imagined. Paul was to arrive in chains for Christ, and even in chains he would feel free to proclaim the Gospel.

In the first chapter of the Letter to the Romans, Paul also says, your faith, the faith of the Church of Rome, is proclaimed in all the world (cf. Rom 1:8). What is memorable about the faith of this Church is that it is proclaimed throughout the world, and we can reflect on the situation today. Today too, a lot is said about the Church of Rome, many things, but let us hope that people are also talking about our faith, about the exemplary faith of this Church, and let us pray the Lord that we may ensure that they do not say many things but speak of the faith of the Church of Rome.

The text that was read (Rom 12:1–2) is the beginning of the fourth and last part of the Letter to the Romans and begins with the word "I appeal to you" (Rom 12:1). It is usually said that it is a question of the moral part that follows the dogmatic part, but in St. Paul's thought and also in his language things cannot be divided in this manner: this word "appeal," in Greek *parakalo*, contains within it the word *paraklesis—parakletos*, it has a depth that goes far beyond morality; it is a term that certainly implies reproof, but also consolation, care for others, fatherly and indeed motherly tenderness; this word "mercy"—in Greek *oiktirmon* and in Hebrew *rachamim*, maternal womb—expresses the compassion, kindness, and tenderness of a mother. And if Paul is making an appeal, all this is implicit: he speaks from the heart, he speaks with the tenderness of a father's love, and it is not only he who speaks. Paul says, "by the mercies of God" (Rom 12:1): he makes himself an instrument of God's words, an instrument of Christ's words; Christ speaks to us with this tenderness, with this fatherly love, with this care for us. And so too he does not only appeal to our morality and our will, but also to the Grace that is in us, an appeal to us to let Grace act. It is, as it were, an action in which the Grace given at Baptism becomes active within us, it must be active within us; thus Grace, the gift of God, and our cooperation go hand in hand.

What is Paul appealing for in this regard? "Present your bodies as a living sacrifice, holy and acceptable to God" (Rom 12:1). "Present your bodies": he speaks of the liturgy, he speaks of God, of the priority of God but he does not speak of the liturgy as a ceremony, he speaks of the liturgy as life. We ourselves, our body; we in our body and as a body must be liturgy. This is the newness of the New Testament, and we shall see it again later: Christ offers himself and thereby replaces all the other sacrifices. And he wants "to draw" us into the communion of his

Body. Our body, with his, becomes God's glory, becomes liturgy. Hence this term "present"—in Greek *parastesai*—is not only an allegory; allegorically our life would also be a liturgy, but, on the contrary, the true liturgy is that of our body, of our being in the Body of Christ, just as Christ himself made the liturgy of the world, the cosmic liturgy, which strives to draw all people to itself.

"In your body, present your body": these words indicate man in his totality, indivisible — in the end—between soul and body, spirit and body; in the body we are ourselves and the body enlivened by the soul, the body itself, must be the realization of our worship. And we think—perhaps, I would say, each one of us should then reflect on these words—that our daily life in our body, in the small things, must be inspired, profuse, immersed in the divine reality, it must become action together with God. This does not mean that we must always be thinking of God, but that we must really be penetrated by the reality of God so that our whole life—and not only a few thoughts—may be a liturgy, may be adoration.

Then Paul tells us, "Present your bodies as a living sacrifice" (Rom 12:1): the Greek term is *logike latreia*, and it then appears in the Roman Canon, in the First Eucharistic Prayer, *"rationabile obsequium."* It is a new definition of worship but is prepared for both in the Old Testament and in Greek philosophy; they are two rivers—so to speak—that flow toward this point and converge in the new liturgy of Christians and of Christ. In the Old Testament: from the outset they understood that God did not need bulls, rams, and such things. In Psalm 50, God says, Do you think I eat the flesh of bulls or drink the blood of goats? I have no need of these things, I do not like them. I do not drink and eat these things. They are not a sacrifice for me. Sacrifice is praise of God, if you come to me it is thanksgiving to God (cf. Ps 50:13-15, 23). Thus the Old Testament route leads toward a point in which these external things, symbols and substitutions, disappear and man himself becomes praise of God.

The same happens in the world of Greek philosophy. Here too one understands increasingly that it is not possible to glorify God with these things—animals or offerings—but that only the "logos" of man, his reason having become the glory of God, is really worship, and the idea is that man must come out of himself and unite with the "Logos," with the great Reason of the world and thus truly be worship. However, here there is something missing: man, according to this philosophy, must—so to speak—leave his body, he must be spiritualized; only the spirit would be adoration. Christianity, on the contrary, is not simply spiritualization or moralization: it is incarnation, that is, Christ is the "Logos"; he is the incarnate Word, and he gathers all of us so that in him and with him, in his Body, as members of this Body, we really become a glorification of God.

Let us keep this in mind: on the one hand, of course, to emerge from these material things for a more spiritual conception of the worship of God, but on the other to arrive at the incarnation of the spirit, to arrive at the point in which our body is assumed into the Body of Christ and our praise of God is not purely words, purely activities, but the reality of our whole life. I think that we must reflect on this and pray to God to help us so that his spirit may take flesh in us, too, and our flesh may become full of God's Spirit.

We also find the same reality in the fourth chapter of St. John's Gospel where the Lord says to the Samaritan woman, in the future people will not worship on this mountain or that, with one rite or another; but they will worship in spirit and in truth (cf. Jn 4:21–23). To come out of these carnal rites is of course spiritualization, but this spirit, this truth, is not any kind of abstract spirit: the spirit is the Holy Spirit, and the truth is Christ. Worshipping in spirit and truth really means to enter through the Holy Spirit into the Body of Christ, into the truth of being. And thus we become truth and we become a glorification of God. Becoming truth in Christ demands our total involvement.

And then let us continue: "Holy and acceptable to God, which is your spiritual worship" (Rom 12:1). The second verse: after this fundamental definition of our life as the liturgy of God, the incarnation of the Word in us, every day, with Christ—the Incarnate Word—St. Paul continues: "Do not be conformed to this world but be transformed by the renewal of your mind" (Rom 12:2). "Do not be conformed to this world." There is the nonconformism of Christians who do not let themselves be conformed. This does not mean that we want to flee from the world, that the world does not interest us: on the contrary, we want to transform ourselves and to let ourselves be transformed, thereby transforming the world. And we must bear in mind that in the New Testament, especially in the Gospel according to St. John, the word "world" has two meanings and thus points to the problem and to the reality concerned. On one side is the "world" created by God, loved by God, to the point that he gives himself and his Son for this world; the world is a creature of God, God loves it and wants to give himself so that it may really be a creation and respond to his love. But there is also the other conception of the "world," *kosmos houtos*: the world that is in evil, that is in the power of evil, that reflects original sin. We see this power of evil today, for example, in two great powers that are useful and good in themselves but can easily be abused: the power of finance and the power of the media. Both are necessary, because they can be useful, but are so easy to abuse that they frequently convey the opposite of their true intentions.

We see that the world of finance can dominate the human being, that possessions and appearance dominate the world and enslave it. The world of finance is no longer an instrument to foster well-being, to foster human life, but becomes a power that oppresses it, that almost demands worship: *"Mammon,"* the real false divinity that dominates the world. To counter this conformism of submission to this power we must be nonconformist: "having" does not count, it is "being" that counts! Let us not submit to the former, let us use it as a means, but with the freedom of God's children.

Then the other, the power of public opinion. Of course we need information, we need knowledge of world affairs, but then it can be a power of appearance; in the end, what is said counts more than the reality itself. An appearance is superimposed on reality, it becomes more important, and man no longer follows the truth of his being, but wishes above all to appear, to be in conformity with these realities. And Christian nonconformism is also against this: we do not always wish "to be conformed," to be praised, we do not want appearances, but the truth, and this gives us freedom and true Christian freedom; in freeing ourselves from this need to please, to speak as the masses think we ought to, in order to have the freedom of truth and thus to rec-reate the world in such a way that it is not oppressed by opinion, by appearances that no longer allow the reality to emerge; the virtual world becomes more real, stronger, and the real world of God's Creation is no longer seen. The nonconformism of the Christian redeems us, restores the truth to us. Let us pray the Lord that he help us to be free people in this nonconformism that is not against the world but is true love of the world.

And St. Paul continues: "Be transformed by the renewal of your mind" (Rom 12:2). Two very important words: "to trans-form," from the Greek *metamorphon*, and "to renew," in Greek *anakainosis*. Transforming ourselves, letting ourselves be trans-formed by the Lord into the form of the image of God, trans-forming ourselves every day anew, through his reality into the truth of our being. And "renewal"; this is the true novelty that does not subject us to opinions, to appearances, but to the Grace of God, to his revelation. Let us permit ourselves to be formed, to be molded, so that the image of God really appears in the human being.

"By the renewal," St. Paul says, in a way I find surprising, "of your mind." Therefore this renewal, this transformation, begins with the renewal of thought. St. Paul says *"o nous"*: our entire way of reasoning, reason itself must be renewed. Renewed not according to the usual categories, but to renew means truly al-lowing ourselves to be illuminated by the Truth that speaks to us in the Word of God. And so, finally, to learn the new way of thinking, which is that way that does not obey power and pos-sessing, appearances, etc., but obeys the truth of our being that dwells in our depths and that is given to us anew in Baptism.

"The renewal of your mind"; every day is a task proper to the process of studying theology, of preparing for the priesthood. Studying theology well, spiritually, thinking about it deeply, meditating on Scripture every day; this way of studying theology, listening to God himself who speaks to us is the way to the renewal of thought, to the transformation of our being and of the world. And lastly, "Let us do everything," according to Paul, "to be able to discern God's will, what is good and acceptable and perfect" (cf. Rom 12:2). Discerning God's will: we can only learn this in a humble and obedient journey with the Word of God, with the Church, with the Sacraments, with meditation on Sacred Scripture. Knowing and discerning God's will, all that is good. This is fundamental in our life.

Moreover on the day of Our Lady of Trust, we see in Our Lady the very reality of all this, the person who is really new, who is really transformed, who is really a living sacrifice. Our Lady sees the will of God, she lives in God's will, she says "yes," and this "yes" of Our Lady is the whole of her being, and thus she shows us the way, she helps us.

Consequently on this day, let us pray to Our Lady who is the living icon of the new man. May she help us to transform, to let our being be transformed, to truly be new men, then later, if God wishes, to be Pastors of his Church. Many thanks.

22. The Source of Every Gift

From *Message of the Holy Father for the 49th World Day
of Prayer for Vocations*, April 29, 2012

The 49th World Day of Prayer for Vocations, which will be celebrated on April 29, 2012, the Fourth Sunday of Easter, prompts us to meditate on the theme *Vocations, the Gift of the Love of God*.

The source of every perfect gift is God who is Love—*Deus Caritas Est*: "Whoever remains in love remains in God and God in him" (1 Jn 4:16). Sacred Scripture tells the story of this original bond between God and man, which precedes creation itself. Writing to the Christians of the city of Ephesus, Saint Paul raises a hymn of gratitude and praise to the Father who, with infinite benevolence, in the course of the centuries accomplishes his universal plan of salvation, which is a plan of love. In his Son Jesus—Paul states—"he chose us, before the foundation of the world, to be holy and without blemish before him in love" (Eph 1:4). We are loved by God even "before" we come into existence! Moved solely by his unconditional love, he created us "not ... out of existing things" (cf. 2 Mc 7:28), to bring us into full communion with Him.

In great wonderment before the work of God's providence, the Psalmist exclaims, "When I see the heavens, the work of your hands, the moon and the stars which you arranged, what is man that you should keep him in mind, mortal man that you care for him?" (Ps 8:3–4). The profound truth of our existence is thus contained in this surprising mystery: every creature, and in particular every human person, is the fruit of God's thought and an act of his love, a love that is boundless, faithful, and everlasting (cf. Jer 31:3). The discovery of this reality is what truly and profoundly changes our lives. In a famous page of the *Confessions*, Saint Augustine expresses with great force his discovery of God, supreme beauty, and supreme love, a God who was always close to him, and to whom he at last opened his mind and heart to be transformed: "Late have I loved you, O Beauty ever ancient, ever new, late have I loved you! You were within me, but I was outside, and it was there that I searched for you. In my unloveliness I plunged into the lovely things which you created. You were with me, but I was not with you. Created things kept me from you; yet if they had not been in you they would have not been at all. You called, you shouted, and you broke through my deafness. You flashed, you shone, and you dispelled my blindness. You breathed your fragrance on me; I drew in breath and now I pant for you. I have tasted you, now I hunger and thirst for more. You touched me, and I burned for your peace."[21] With these images, the Saint of Hippo seeks to describe the ineffable mystery of his encounter with God, with God's love that transforms all of life.

It is a love that is limitless and that precedes us, sustains us, and calls us along the path of life, a love rooted in an absolutely free gift of God. Speaking particularly of the ministerial priesthood, my predecessor, Blessed John Paul II, stated that "every ministerial action—while it leads to loving and serving the Church—provides an incentive to grow in ever greater love and service of Jesus Christ the head, shepherd and spouse of the Church, a love

21. Augustine, *Confessions*, trans. Henry Chadwick (New York: Oxford University Press, 2008), 10.

which is always a response to the free and unsolicited love of God in Christ."²² Every specific vocation is in fact born of the initiative of God; *it is a gift of the Love of God!* He is the One who takes the "first step," and not because he has found something good in us, but because of the presence of his own love "poured out into our hearts through the Holy Spirit" (Rom 5:5).

In every age, the source of the divine call is to be found in the initiative of the infinite love of God, who reveals himself fully in Jesus Christ. As I wrote in my first Encyclical, *Deus Caritas Est*, "God is indeed visible in a number of ways. In the love-story recounted by the Bible, he comes towards us, he seeks to win our hearts, all the way to the Last Supper, to the piercing of his heart on the Cross, to his appearances after the Resurrection and to the great deeds by which, through the activity of the Apostles, he guided the nascent Church along its path. Nor has the Lord been absent from subsequent Church history: he encounters us ever anew, in the men and women who reflect his presence, in his word, in the sacraments, and especially in the Eucharist."²³

The love of God is everlasting; he is faithful to himself, to the "word that he commanded for a thousand generations" (Ps 105:8). Yet the appealing beauty of this divine love, which precedes and accompanies us, needs to be proclaimed ever anew, especially to younger generations. This divine love is the hidden impulse, the motivation that never fails, even in the most difficult circumstances.

Dear brothers and sisters, we need to open our lives to this

22. Cf. Pope John Paul II, Apostolic Exhortation *Pastores Dabo Vobis*, no. 25.
23. Pope Benedict XVI, Encyclical Letter *Deus Caritas Est*, no. 17.

love. It is to the perfection of the Father's love (cf. Mt 5:48) that Jesus Christ calls us every day! The high standard of the Christian life consists in loving "as" God loves, with a love that is shown in the total, faithful, and fruitful gift of self. Saint John of the Cross, writing to the Prioress of the Monastery of Segovia, who was pained by the terrible circumstances surrounding his suspension, responded by urging her to act as God does: "Think nothing else but that God ordains all, and where there is no love, put love, and there you will draw out love."[24]

It is in this soil of self-offering and openness to the love of God, and as the fruit of that love, that all vocations are born and grow. By drawing from this wellspring through prayer, constant recourse to God's word, and to the sacraments, especially the Eucharist, it becomes possible to live a life of love for our neighbors, in whom we come to perceive the face of Christ the Lord (cf. Mt 25:31–46). To express the inseparable bond that links these "two loves"—love of God and love of neighbor—both of which flow from the same divine source and return to it, Pope Saint Gregory the Great uses the metaphor of the seedling: "In the soil of our heart God first planted the root of love for him; from this, like the leaf, sprouts love for one another."[25]

These two expressions of the one divine love must be lived with a particular intensity and purity of heart by those who have decided to set out on the path of vocation discernment toward the ministerial priesthood and the consecrated life; they

24. St. John of the Cross, *Collected Works of St. John of the Cross*, trans. Kieran Kavanaugh and Otilio Rodriguez (Washington, D.C.: ICS, 1991), 22.

25. Gregory the Great, *Moralium Libri Sive Expositio In Librum Beati Job. Pars I* 7:24, *Patrologia Cursus Completus*, PL, 75:780.

are its distinguishing mark. Love of God, which priests and consecrated persons are called to mirror, however imperfectly, is the motivation for answering the Lord's call to special consecration through priestly ordination or the profession of the evangelical counsels. Saint Peter's vehement reply to the Divine Master: "Yes, Lord, you know that I love you" (Jn 21:15) contains the secret of a life fully given and lived out, and thus one that is deeply joyful.

The other practical expression of love, that toward our neighbor, and especially those who suffer and are in greatest need, is the decisive impulse that leads the priest and the consecrated person to be a sower of hope and a builder of communion between people. The relationship of consecrated persons, and especially of the priest, to the Christian community is vital and becomes a fundamental dimension of their affectivity. The Curé of Ars was fond of saying, "Priests are not priests for themselves, but for you."[26]

Dear brother bishops, dear priests, deacons, consecrated men and women, catechists, pastoral workers, and all of you who are engaged in the field of educating young people: I fervently exhort you to pay close attention to those members of parish communities, associations, and ecclesial movements who sense a call to the priesthood or to a special consecration. It is important for the Church to create the conditions that will permit many young people to say "yes" in generous response to God's loving call.

The task of fostering vocations will be to provide helpful

26. Alfred Monnin, *Life of the Curé d'Ars* (London: Burns and Lambert, 1862), 281.

guidance and direction along the way. Central to this should be love of God's word nourished by a growing familiarity with sacred Scripture and attentive and unceasing prayer, both personal and in community; this will make it possible to hear God's call amid all the voices of daily life. But above all, the Eucharist should be the heart of every vocational journey: it is here that the love of God touches us in Christ's sacrifice, the perfect expression of love, and it is here that we learn ever anew how to live according to the "high standard" of God's love. Scripture, prayer, and the Eucharist are the precious treasure enabling us to grasp the beauty of a life spent fully in service of the Kingdom.

It is my hope that the local Churches and all the various groups within them will become places where vocations are carefully discerned and their authenticity tested, places where young men and women are offered wise and strong spiritual direction. In this way, the Christian community itself becomes a manifestation of the Love of God in which every calling is contained. As a response to the demands of the new commandment of Jesus, this can find eloquent and particular realization in Christian families, whose love is an expression of the love of Christ who gave himself for his Church (cf. Eph 5:32). Within the family, "a community of life and love,"[27] young people can have a wonderful experience of this self-giving love. Indeed, families are not only the privileged place for human and Christian formation; they can also be "the primary and most excellent seed-bed of vocations to a life of consecration to the Kingdom

---

27. Second Vatican Council, Pastoral Constitution *Gaudium et Spes*, no. 48.

of God"[28] by helping their members to see, precisely within the family, the beauty and the importance of the priesthood and the consecrated life. May pastors and all the lay faithful always co-operate so that in the Church these "homes and schools of communion" may multiply, modeled on the Holy Family of Nazareth, the harmonious reflection on earth of the life of the Most Holy Trinity.

With this prayerful hope, I cordially impart my Apostolic Blessing to all of you: my brother bishops, priests, deacons, religious men and women, and all lay faithful, and especially those young men and women who strive to listen with a docile heart to God's voice and are ready to respond generously and faithfully.

28. Pope John Paul II, Apostolic Exhortation *Familiaris Consortio* (November 22, 1981), no. 53.

PART 3

THE MEANING OF SEMINARY
FORMATION

23. With Mary and Joseph

From *Address of His Holiness Benedict XVI*, Roman Major
Seminary, February 25, 2006

It gives me great pleasure to be with you this evening at the Roman Major Seminary on such a special occasion as the Feast of your Patroness, Our Lady of Trust.

I have long been awaiting an opportunity to come in person to visit you who make up the community of the Seminary, one of the most important places in the Diocese. There are many seminaries in Rome but this one, strictly speaking, is the Diocesan Seminary, as is recalled by its location here in the Lateran, next to the Cathedral of St. John, the Cathedral of Rome.

Consequently, following a tradition dear to beloved Pope John Paul II, I have made the most of today's feast to meet you here, where you pray, study, and live in brotherhood, training for your future pastoral ministry.

It really is very beautiful and meaningful that you venerate the Virgin Mary, Mother of Priests, with the special title of *Our Lady of Trust*. It evokes a twofold meaning: the trust of the Seminarians who, with her help, set out on their journey in response to Christ who has called them, and the trust of the Church of Rome (especially that of her Bishop), which invokes the protection of Mary, the Mother of every vocation, upon this nursery-garden of priests.

It is with Mary's help, dear Seminarians, that today you can prepare for your mission as priests at the service of the Church. A moment ago, when I paused in prayer before the venerable image of Our Lady of Trust in your Chapel, which is the heart of your Seminary, I prayed for each one of you. In the meantime, I was thinking once again of the many seminarians who have passed through the Roman Seminary and have subsequently served Christ's Church with love. I am thinking among others of Fr. Andrea Santoro, recently killed in Turkey while he was praying. And I also called upon the Mother of the Redeemer to obtain for you the gift of holiness. May the Holy Spirit, who shaped the priestly Heart of Jesus in the Virgin's womb and later at the house in Nazareth, work within you with his grace, preparing you for the future tasks that will be entrusted to you.

It is equally beautiful and appropriate today that together with the Virgin Mother of Trust, we should venerate in a special way her husband, St. Joseph, who has inspired Msgr. Marco Frisina's Oratory this year. I thank him for his sensitivity, for having chosen to honor my holy Patron, and I congratulate him on this composition, while I warmly thank the soloists, the choir, the organist, and all the members of the orchestra.

This Oratory, significantly entitled *Shadow of the Father*, affords me an opportunity to emphasize how the example of St. Joseph, a "just man," the Evangelist says, fully responsible before God and before Mary, should be an encouragement to all of you on your way toward the priesthood.

Joseph appears to us ever attentive to the voice of the Lord, who guides the events of history, and ready to follow the instructions, ever faithful, generous, and detached in service, an effective teacher of prayer and of work in the hidden life at Nazareth. I can assure you, dear Seminarians, that the further you advance with God's grace on the path of the priesthood, the more you will experience what abundant spiritual fruits result from calling on St. Joseph and invoking his support in carrying out your daily duty.

Dear Seminarians, please accept my most cordial best wishes for your present and your future. I place them in the hands of Mary Most Holy, Our Lady of Trust. May those who are formed at the Roman Major Seminary learn to repeat the beautiful invocation Mater mea, fiducia mea, your distinctive motto that was coined by my Venerable Predecessor Benedict XV.

I pray that these words will be impressed upon the hearts of each one of you and will accompany you always, in your life and in your priestly ministry. Thus, you will be able to spread around you, wherever you may be, the fragrance of Mary's trust that is trust in God's provident and faithful love.

24. Growing in Holiness

From *Address of His Holiness Benedict XVI to the Students of the Almo Collegio Capranica*, Sala Clementina, January 20, 2006

Dear young men, the College's organization helps you to prepare yourselves in the best way for your future pastoral mission: prayer, recollection, study, community life, and the support of the formation staff. You can benefit from the fact that your Seminary, rich in history, is integrated into the life of the Diocese of Rome, and the cultivation of its strong bond of fidelity to the Bishop of Rome has always been a commitment and the boast of the Capranica Family.

Moreover, the possibility of doing your theological studies in this City also affords you a special opportunity for growth and openness to the needs of the universal Church. May it be your concern in these years to make the most of every occasion to witness effectively to the Gospel among the people of our time.

To respond to the expectations of modern society and cooperate in the vast evangelizing action that involves all Christians, we need well-trained and courageous priests who are free from ambition and fear but convinced of the Gospel's Truth, whose chief concern is to proclaim Christ and who are prepared to stoop down to suffering humanity in his Name, enabling everyone, particularly the poor and all who are in difficulty, to experience the comfort of God's love and the warmth of the ecclesial family.

As you well know, in addition to human maturity and persevering adherence to the revealed truth that is faithfully presented by the Church's Magisterium, this entails a serious commitment to personal holiness and the practice of the virtues, especially humility and charity; you must also foster communion with the various members of the People of God, so that in each one of you the awareness of being part of the one Body of Christ and members one of another (cf. Rom 12:4–6) may grow.

To achieve this, dear friends, I ask you to keep your eyes fixed on Christ, the Author and Perfecter of faith (cf. Heb 12:2). Indeed, the greater your communion with him, the better able you will be to follow faithfully in his footsteps, so that, under the guidance of the Holy Spirit, your love for the Lord will develop in "love, which binds everything together in perfect harmony" (Col 3:14).

You have before your eyes the testimonies of zealous priests whom your "Almo" College has listed among its alumnae through the years, priests who contributed a wealth of knowledge and goodness to the Lord's Vineyard. Follow their example!

Dear friends, the Pope accompanies you with prayer, asking the Lord to comfort you and to fill you with abundant gifts. May St. Agnes, who, at a young age, resisting flattery and threats, chose as her treasure the precious "pearl" of the Kingdom and loved Christ to the point of martyrdom, intercede for you. May the Virgin Mary obtain that you bear abundant fruits of good deeds, in praise of the Lord and for the good of the Holy Church.

To seal these hopes, I impart with affection my Apostolic Blessing to you and to the entire Community of the Capranica, and I willingly extend it to all your loved ones.

25. Confronting the Challenges of the World

From *Address of His Holiness Benedict XVI to a Group of Priests and Seminarians from the Theological College of the* "APOSTOLIKI DIAKONIA" *of the Greek Orthodox Church*, Consistory Hall, February 27, 2006

As I welcome you with joy and gratitude on the occasion of the initiative of this visit to Rome, I would like to recall an exhortation that St. Ignatius, the great Bishop of Antioch, addressed to the Ephesians: *"Take pains to meet more often to give thanks to God and to celebrate his praise. For if you meet frequently, the forces of evil will be overcome and his work of death will be destroyed by the harmony of your faith."*[1]

At the beginning of the second millennium, for us Christians of East and West, the forces of evil have also acted in the controversies between us that still endure.

In the past forty years, however, many comforting signs full of hope have allowed us to glimpse a new dawn, that of the day on which we will fully understand that being rooted and founded in the love of Christ actually means finding a practical way to overcome our divisions through personal and community conversion, the practice of listening to each other, and common prayer for our unity.

Among the consoling signs on this journey, which is demanding but indispensable, I would like to recall the recent positive development of relations between the Church of Rome and the Orthodox Church of Greece. Various forms of collaboration and projects that serve to deepen our understanding of one another and to foster the formation of the youngest generations have followed the memorable meeting on the Areopagus of Athens between my beloved Predecessor, Pope John Paul II, and His Beatitude Christodoulos, Archbishop of Athens and All Greece.

The exchange of visits, scholarship, and cooperation in the editorial field have proven to be an effective means of furthering dialogue and deepening charity, which is the perfection of life and—as St. Ignatius also said,—together with the principle, faith, will be able to prevail over the discord of this world.

I warmly thank the *Apostoliki Diakonia* for this visit to Rome

---

1. Ignatius of Antioch, *The Epistles*, ed. Paul A. Boer Sr. (CreateSpace Independent Publishing Platform, 2012), 68.

and for the initiatives of formation that it is developing with the *Catholic Committee for Cultural Collaboration* with the Orthodox Churches in the context of the Pontifical Council for Promoting Christian Unity. I am certain that reciprocal charity will be able to foster our creativity and lead us along new paths.

We must confront the challenges that threaten faith, cultivate the spiritual *humus* that has nourished Europe for centuries, reaffirm Christian values, promote peace and encounter, even in the most difficult conditions, and deepen those elements of faith and ecclesial life that can lead us to the goal of full communion in truth and in charity, especially now that the official dialogue between the Catholic Church and the Orthodox Church as a whole is resuming its journey with renewed vigor.

In Christian life, faith, hope, and charity go hand in hand. Our witness in today's world will be truer and more effective if we realize that the way toward unity demands of all of us more living faith, sounder hope, and charity, which is truly the deepest inspiration that nourishes our reciprocal relations! Hope, however, should be practiced with patience and humility, and with trust in the One who guides us.

Although it may not seem within our immediate reach, the goal of unity among Christ's disciples does not prevent us from living with one another in charity at all levels, from this moment. There is no place or time in which love modeled on the love of our Teacher, Jesus, is superfluous; love cannot fail to be a shortcut to full communion.

I entrust to you the task of conveying my sentiments of sincere brotherly love to His Beatitude Christodoulos. He was with us here in Rome to say the last farewell to Pope John Paul II. The

Lord will point out to us the ways and times to renew our encounter in the joyful atmosphere of a meeting among brothers.

26. *Being and Doing*

From *Address of His Holiness Benedict XVI to the Pontifical Lateran University*, October 21, 2006

EXTEMPORANEOUS GREETING
ON HIS ARRIVAL

I am happy to be here in "my" University, because this is the University of the Bishop of Rome. I know that here the truth is sought, and so ultimately, Christ is sought, because he is the Truth in person. This journey toward the truth—trying to know the truth better in all of its expressions—is in reality a fundamental ecclesial service.

A great Belgian theologian wrote a book, *Love of the Arts and the Desire of God*, and has shown that in the monastic tradition the two things go together, because God is Word and speaks to us through Scripture. Therefore, suppose that we begin to read, study, and deepen the knowledge of the Arts, and thus deepen our knowledge of the Word.

In this sense, the opening of the Library is both an academic, university event and a spiritual, theological event, precisely because through reading, on the path toward the truth, studying the words to find the Word, we are at the service of the Lord. A service of the Gospel for the world, because the world needs the truth. There is no freedom without truth; [without it] we are not in total harmony with the original idea of the Creator.

Thank you for your work! May the Lord bless you in this Academic Year.

I recall my last Visit to the Lateran with pleasure and, as if time had not elapsed, I would like to take up again the theme then under discussion, almost as though we had been interrupted only for a few seconds.

A context such as the academic one invites in its peculiar way to enter anew the theme of the crisis of culture and identity, which in these decades dramatically places itself before our eyes.

The University is one of the best-qualified places to attempt to find opportune ways to exit from this situation. In the University, in fact, the wealth of tradition that remains alive through the centuries is preserved in it (and especially the Library is an essential means to safeguard the richness of tradition) and can be illustrated in the fecundity of the truth when it is welcomed in its authenticity with a simple and open soul.

In the University the young generations are formed who await a serious, demanding proposal, capable of responding in new contexts to the perennial question on the meaning of our existence. This expectation must not be disappointed.

The contemporary context seems to give primacy to an artificial intelligence that becomes ever more dominated by experimental techniques and in this way forgets that all science must always safeguard man and promote his aspiration for the authentic good.

To overrate "doing," obscuring "being," does not help to recompose the fundamental balance that everyone needs in order to give his own existence a solid foundation and valid goal.

Every man, in fact, is called to give meaning to his own actions, above all when this is put in the perspective of a scientific discovery that weakens the very essence of personal life.

To let oneself be taken up by the taste for discovery without safeguarding the criteria that come from a more profound vision would be to fall easily into the drama of which an ancient myth speaks: Young Icarus, exhilarated by the flight toward absolute freedom and heedless of the warning of his old father, Daedalus, flew ever nearer to the sun, forgetting that the wings with which he flew in the sky were made of wax. His violent fall and death were the price of his illusion.

The ancient fable has a perennially valid lesson. In life there are other illusions that one cannot trust without risking disastrous consequences for the existence of one's self and others.

The university professor has the duty not only to investigate the truth and to arouse perennial wonder from it, but also to foster its knowledge in every facet and to defend it from reductive and distorted interpretations.

To make the theme of truth central is not merely a speculative act, restricted to a small circle of thinkers; on the contrary, it is a vital question in order to give a more profound identity to personal life and to heighten responsibility in social relations (cf. Eph 4:25).

In fact, if the question of the truth and the concrete possibility for every person to be able to reach it is neglected, life ends up being reduced to a plethora of hypotheses, deprived of assurances and points of reference.

As the famous humanist, Erasmus, once said, "Opinions are the source of happiness at a cheap price! To understand the true essence of things, even if it treats of things of minimal importance, costs great endeavor."[2]

It is this endeavor that the University must commit itself to accomplish; it passes through study and research in a spirit of patient perseverance. This endeavor, however, enables one to enter progressively into the heart of questions and to open oneself to passion for the truth and to the joy of finding it.

The words of the holy Bishop Anselm of Aosta remain totally current: "That I may seek you desiring you, that I may desire you seeking you, that I may find you loving you, and that loving you I may find you again."[3]

May the space of silence and contemplation, which are the indispensable background upon which to gather the questions the mind raises, find within these walls attentive persons who know how to value the importance, the efficacy, and the consequences for personal and social living.

God is the ultimate truth to whom all reason naturally tends, solicited by the desire to totally fulfill the journey assigned to it. God is not an empty word or an abstract hypothesis; on the contrary, he is the foundation upon which to build one's life.

To live in the world *"veluti si Deus daretur"* brings with it the assumption of a responsibility that knows how to be concerned with investigating every feasible route in order to come as near as possible to him who is the goal toward which everything tends (cf. 1 Cor 15:24).

The believer knows that this God has a Face and that Once for All, with Jesus Christ, he has drawn near to each man.

2. Cf. Desiderius Erasmus, *The Praise of Folly* XL.VII.
3. Cf. Anselm of Aosta, *Proslogion* 1.

The Second Vatican Council acutely recalled this: "For, by his Incarnation, he, the Son of God, has in a certain way united himself with each man. He worked with human hands, he thought with a human mind. He acted with a human will, and with a human heart he loved. Born of the Virgin Mary, he has truly been made one of us, like to us in all things except sin."[4] To know him is to know the full truth, thanks to which one can find freedom: "You will know the truth, and the truth will make you free" (Jn 8:32).

27. *Listening to God*

From *Address of His Holiness Benedict XVI to the Pontifical Gregorian University*, November 3, 2006

I am pleased to meet with you today. My first greeting goes precisely to you students, whom I see in large numbers in this elegant and austere interior quadrangle, but whom I know are also gathered in various halls and are in contact with us by means of screens and loudspeakers.

Dear young people, I thank you for the sentiments expressed by your representative and by you yourselves. In a certain sense, the University is truly yours. It has existed since St. Ignatius founded it for you, for students, long ago in 1551.

All the energy that your Professors and Lecturers expend in teaching and research is for you. The daily efforts and worries of the Rector Magnificent, the Vice-Rectors, the Deans, and the

4. Second Vatican Council, Dogmatic Constitution *Gaudium et Spes*, no. 22.

Provosts are for you. You are aware of this, and I am sure that you are also grateful to them for it.

I then offer a special greeting to Cardinal Zenon Grocholewski. As Prefect of the Congregation for Catholic Education, he is Grand Chancellor of this University and represents the Roman Pontiff in it.[5]

For this very reason, my Predecessor Pius XI, of venerable memory, declared the Gregorian University "Pontifical: *"plenissimo iure ac nomi."*[6]

The actual history of the *Roman College* and of its heir, the Gregorian University, as the Rector said in his tribute to me, forms the basis of these very special Statutes.

I greet Fr. Peter-Hans Kolvenbach, SJ, who as Superior General of the Society of Jesus is Grand Chancellor of the University and most directly concerned with this work, which I do not hesitate to describe as one of the greatest services that the Society of Jesus carries out for the universal Church.

I greet the benefactors who are present here: the *Freundeskreis der Gregoriana* from Germany, the *Gregorian University Foundation* from New York, the *Fondazione La Gregoriana* of Rome, and other groups of benefactors.

Dear friends, I am grateful to you for all that you generously do to support this institution, which the Holy See has entrusted and continues to entrust to the Society of Jesus.

I greet the Jesuit Fathers who carry out their teaching here with a praiseworthy spirit of self-denial and austerity of life;

5. Pontifical Gregorian University, *Statuta Universitatis, art.* 6, 2.

6. Pope Pius XI, Apostolic Letter *Gregorianam Studiorum* (June 21, 1932): Acta Apostolicae Sedis 24 (1932), 268.

with them I greet the other Lecturers and extend my thoughts to the Fathers and Brothers of the Pontifical Biblical Institute and the Pontifical Oriental Institute.

Together with the Gregorian University, they form a prestigious academic *consortium*,[7] since it covers not only teaching but also the patrimony of books of the three libraries, which include incomparable specialized collections.

Lastly, I greet the nonteaching personnel of the University who have wished to make their own voice heard through that of the General Secretary, whom I thank. The nonteaching staff daily carries out a hidden service, but one very important to the mission that the mandate of the Holy See requires of the Gregorian; I offer my cordial encouragement to each one of them.

I am delighted to be in this quadrangle, which I have crossed on various occasions. I remember in particular the defense of the thesis of Fr. Lohfink during the Council in the presence of many Cardinals and also of humble experts like myself.

I am especially fond of recalling the time in 1972 when, as Professor of Dogmatics and the History of Dogma at the University of Regensburg, I was sent by the then Rector, Fr. Hervé Carrier, SJ, to give a course to students of the second cycle specializing in Dogmatic Theology. I gave a course on the Most Holy Eucharist.

With the familiarity of those times, I can tell you, dear Professors and students, that if the effort of study and teaching is to have any meaning in relation to God's Kingdom, it must be sustained by the theological virtues. In fact, the immediate ob-

---

7. Pope Pius XI, Motu Proprio *Quod Maxime* (September 30, 1928).

ject of the different branches of theological knowledge is God himself, revealed in Jesus Christ, God with a human face.

Even when, as in Canon Law and in Church History, the immediate object is the People of God in its visible, historical dimension, the deeper analysis of the topic urges us once again to contemplation, in the faith, of the mystery of the Risen Christ. It is he, present in his Church, who leads her among the events of the time toward eschatological fullness, a goal to which we have set out sustained by hope.

However, knowing God is not enough. For a true encounter with him one must also love him. Knowledge must become love.

The study of Theology, Canon Law, and Church History is not only knowledge of the propositions of the faith in their historical formulation and practical application, but is also always knowledge of them in faith, hope, and charity.

The Spirit alone searches the depths of God (cf. 1 Cor 2:10); thus, only in listening to the Spirit can one search the depths of the riches, wisdom, and knowledge of God (cf. Rom 11:33).

We listen to the Spirit in prayer, when the heart opens to contemplation of God's mystery, which was revealed to us in Jesus Christ the Son, image of the invisible God (cf. Col 1:15), constituted Head of the Church and Lord of all things (cf. Eph 1:10; Col 1:18).

Since its origins as the *Collegium Romanum*, the Gregorian University has been distinguished for the study of philosophy and theology. It would take too long to list the names of the outstanding philosophers and theologians who have followed one another in the Chairs of this academic Centre; we should also add to them those of the famous canon lawyers and Church historians who expended their energies within these prestigious walls.

They all made a substantial contribution to the progress of the branches of knowledge they studied, hence, they offered a precious service to the Apostolic See in the exercise of its doctrinal, disciplinary, and pastoral role. With the development of the times, outlooks necessarily change.

Today, one must take into account the confrontation with secular culture in many parts of the world, which not only tends to deny every sign of God's presence in the life of society and of the individual, but, with various means that bewilder and cloud the upright human conscience, is seeking to corrode the human being's capacity and readiness to listen to God.

Moreover, it is impossible to ignore relations with other religions, which will only prove constructive if we avoid all forms of ambiguity, which in a certain way undermine the essential content of Christian faith in Christ, the one Savior of all mankind (cf. Acts 4:12), and in the Church, the necessary sacrament of salvation for all humanity.[8]

Here, I cannot forget the other human sciences that are encouraged at this famous University in the wake of the glorious academic tradition of the Roman College. The great prestige the Roman College acquired in the fields of mathematics, physics, and astronomy is well known to all.

It suffices to remember that the "Gregorian" Calendar, so-called because it was desired by my Predecessor Gregory XIII,

---

8. Cf. Congregation for the Doctrine of the Faith, Declaration *Dominus Iesus* (August 6, 2000), no. 3.

and currently in use throughout the world, was compiled in 1582 by Fr. Christopher Clavius, a Lecturer at the Roman College. It suffices also to mention Fr. Matteo Ricci, who took to as far as distant China the knowledge he had acquired as a disciple of Fr. Clavius, in addition to his witness to the faith.

Today, the above-mentioned disciplines are no longer taught at the Gregorian University, but have been replaced by other human sciences such as psychology, the social sciences, and social communications.

Thus, man desires to be more deeply understood, both in his profound personal dimension and his external dimension as a builder of society in justice and peace, and as a communicator of the truth.

For the very reason that these sciences concern the human being, they cannot set aside reference to God. In fact, man, both in his interiority and in his exteriority, cannot be fully understood unless he recognizes that he is open to transcendence.

Deprived of his reference to God, man cannot respond to the fundamental questions that trouble and will always trouble his heart concerning the end of his life, hence, also its meaning. As a result, it is no longer possible to introduce into society those ethical values that alone can guarantee a coexistence worthy of man.

Human destiny without reference to God cannot but be the desolation of anguish, which leads to desperation.

Only in reference to God's Love that is revealed in Jesus Christ can man find the meaning of his existence and live in hope, even if he must face evils that injure his personal existence and the society in which he lives.

Hope ensures that man does not withdraw into a paralyzing

and sterile nihilism but opens himself instead to generous commitment within the society where he lives in order to improve it. This is the task that God entrusted to man when he created him in his own image and likeness, a task that fills every human being with the greatest possible dignity, but also with an immense responsibility.

It is in this perspective that you, Professors and Lecturers at the Gregorian, are called to train the students whom the Church entrusts to you. The integral formation of young people has been one of the traditional apostolates of the Society of Jesus since its origins; this is why the Roman College took on this mission at the outset.

The entrustment to the Society of Jesus in Rome, close to the Apostolic See, of The [Pontifical] German College, The Roman Seminary, The German-Hungarian College, The English College, The Greek College, The Scots College, and The Irish College, was intended to ensure the formation of the clergy of those nations where the unity of the faith and communion with the Apostolic See had been broken.

These Colleges still send almost all their students or large numbers of them to the Gregorian University, in continuity with that original mission.

Down through history, many other Colleges have joined those mentioned above, so the task that weighs heavily upon your shoulders, dear Professors and Lecturers, is more demanding than ever!

Appropriately, therefore, after deep reflection, you have drafted a "Declaration of Intentions" that is essential for an institution like yours, since it sums up its nature and its mission.

On this basis you are nearing the conclusion of your revision of the Statutes of the University and of the General Rules, as well as of the Statutes and Rules of the various Faculties, Institutes, and Centers.

This will help to define the identity of the Gregorian more clearly and allow for the drafting of academic programs better suited to the fulfillment of your mission, which is at the same time both easy and difficult.

It is easy because the identity and mission of the Gregorian have been clear since its earliest days, on the basis of the indications reaffirmed by so many Roman Pontiffs, of whom at least sixteen were students at this University.

At the same time, it is a difficult mission because it implies constant fidelity to its own history and tradition, so as not to lose its historical roots, and openness to contemporary reality to respond creatively, after attentive discernment, to the needs of the Church and the world today.

As a Pontifical Ecclesiastical University, this academic Centre is committed to *sentire in Ecclesia et cum Ecclesia*. It is a commitment born from love for the Church, our Mother and the Bride of Christ. We must love her as Christ himself loved her, assuming the suffering of the world to complete what is lacking in Christ's afflictions in our own flesh (cf. Col 1:24).

In this way, it will be possible to form new generations of priests, Religious, and committed lay people. Indeed, it is only right to ask ourselves what type of formation we wish to impart to our students, whether priest, Religious, or lay person.

Dear Professors and Lecturers, it is of course your intention to form priests who are learned but at the same time prepared to spend their lives serving all those whom the Lord entrusts to their ministry with an undivided heart, in humility and in austerity of life.

Thus, you intend to offer a solid intellectual training to men and women religious, so that they will be able to joyfully live the consecration God has given to them and to offer themselves as an eschatological sign of that future life to which we are all called.

Likewise, you wish to prepare competent lay men and women who will be able to carry out services and offices in the Church, and first and foremost, to be leaven of the Kingdom of God in the temporal sphere.

In this perspective, this very year, the University has initiated an interdisciplinary program to train lay people to live their specifically ecclesial vocation of ethical commitment in the public arena.

However, formation is also your responsibility, dear students. There is no doubt that studying demands constant ascesis and self-denial, but it is precisely on this path that the person is trained in self-denial and the sense of duty.

In fact, what you learn today is what you will communicate tomorrow, when the sacred ministry or other services and offices for the benefit of the community will have been entrusted to you by the Church. What in all circumstances will give joy to your hearts will be the knowledge that you have always fostered upright intentions, thanks to which one may be certain of having sought and done the will of God alone. Obviously, all these things require a purification of the heart and discernment.

Dear sons of St. Ignatius, once again the Pope entrusts to

you this University, such an important institution for the universal Church and for so many particular Churches. It has always been a priority among the priorities of the apostolates of the Society of Jesus. It was in the university environment of Paris that St. Ignatius of Loyola and his first companions developed the ardent desire to help souls by loving and serving God in all things, for his greater glory.

Impelled by the inner promptings of the Spirit, St. Ignatius came to Rome, center of Christianity, the See of the Successor of Peter, to found the *Collegium Romanum* here, the first University of the Society of Jesus.

Today, the Gregorian University is the university environment in which, even after 456 years, the desire of St. Ignatius and his first companions to help souls to love and serve God in all things for his greater glory is being fulfilled.

I would say that here, within these walls, is achieved what Pope Julius III said on July 21, 1550, established in the *"formula Istituti,"* establishing that every member of the Society of Jesus was bound to *"sub crucis vexillo Deo militare, et soli Domino ac Ecclesiae Ipsius sponsae, sub Romano Pontifice, Christi in terris Vicario, servire,"* committing himself *"potissimum ... ad fidei defensionem et propagationem, et profectum animarum in vita et doctrina christiana, per publicas praedicationes, lectiones et aliud quodcumque verbi Dei ministerium."*[9]

This charismatic specificity of the Society of Jesus, expressed institutionally in the fourth vow of total availability to the Roman Pontiff in anything he may see fit to command *"ad profec-*

9. Julius III, Apostolic Letter *Exposcit Debitum* (July 21, 1550), no. 1.

tum animarum et fidei propagationem,"[10] is also evident in the fact that the Superior General of the Company of Jesus summons from across the world the Jesuits best suited to carrying out the task of teaching at this University.

Knowing that this might involve the sacrifice of other works and services to further the aims the Society proposes to achieve, the Church is deeply grateful to it and desires the Gregorian to preserve the Ignatian spirit that enlivens it, expressed in its pedagogical method and curriculum.

Dear friends, with fatherly affection, I entrust all of you who are the living stones of the Gregorian University—Professors and Lecturers, students, nonteaching staff, benefactors, and friends—to the intercession of St. Ignatius of Loyola, St. Robert Bellarmine, and the Blessed Virgin Mary, Queen of the Society of Jesus, who is referred to in the University's coat of arms with the title *Sedes Sapientiae.*

28. *The Life in the Seminary*

From *Address of His Holiness Benedict XVI, Roman Major Seminary,* February 17, 2007

Gregorpaolo Stano, Diocese of Oria (First-Year Philosophy):

Your Holiness, ours is the first of two years dedicated to discernment, during which we are taught to make a profound personal examination. It is a tiring exercise for us, because the language of God is special, and only those who are attentive are

10. Ibid., no. 3.

able to discern it among the thousands of voices clamoring inside us. We are asking you, therefore, to help us to understand how God talks in practice and what clues he gives you in his private pronouncements.

Pope Benedict XVI:

As a first word, a "thank you" to Monsignor Rector for his address. I am already curious to read that text you will be writing and also to learn from it. I am not sure whether I can clarify the essential points of life in the seminary, but I shall give it a try.

Now, for the first question: how can we distinguish God's voice from among the thousands of voices we hear each day in our world? I would say, God speaks with us in many different ways. He speaks through others, through friends, parents, pastors, priests. Here, the priests to whom you are entrusted, who are guiding you.

He speaks by means of the events in our life, in which we are able to discern God's touch; he speaks also through nature, creation, and he speaks, naturally and above all, through his Word, in Sacred Scripture, read in the communion of the Church and read personally in conversation with God.

It is important to read Sacred Scripture in a very personal way, and really, as St. Paul says, not as a human word or a document from the past as we read Homer or Virgil, but as God's Word that is ever timely and speaks to me. It is important to learn to understand in a historical text, a text from the past, the living Word of God, that is, to enter into prayer and thus read Sacred Scripture as a conversation with God.

St. Augustine often says in his homilies, I knocked on various occasions at the door of this Word until I could perceive what God himself was saying to me. It is of paramount importance to combine this very personal reading, this personal talk with God in which I search for what the Lord is saying to me, and in addition to this personal reading, reading it in the community is very important because the living subject of Sacred Scripture is the People of God, it is the Church.

This Scripture was not simply restricted to great writers—even if the Lord always needs the person and his personal response—but it developed with people who were traveling together on the journey of the People of God, and thus, their words are expressions of this journey, of this reciprocity of God's call and the human response. Thus, the subject lives today as it lived at that time so that Scripture does not belong to the past, because its subject, the People of God inspired by this same God, is always the same, and therefore the Word is always alive in the living subject.

It is consequently important to read Sacred Scripture and experience Sacred Scripture in the communion of the Church, that is, with all the great witnesses of this Word, beginning with the first Fathers and ending with today's Saints, with today's Magisterium.

Above all, it is a Word that becomes vital and alive in the Liturgy. I would say, therefore, that the Liturgy is the privileged place where every one of us can enter into the "we" of the sons of God, in conversation with God. This is important. The Our Father begins with the words "Our Father"; only if I am integrated into the "we" of this "Our" can I find the Father; only within this "we," which is the subject of the prayer of the Our Father, do we hear the Word of God clearly.

Thus, this seems to me most important: the Liturgy is the privileged place where the Word is alive, is present, indeed, where the Word, the *Logos*, the Lord, speaks to us and gives himself into our hands; if we are ready to listen to the Lord in this great communion of the Church of all times, we find him. He opens the door to us little by little. I would say, therefore, that this is the focus for all the other points: we are personally directed on our journey by the Lord, and at the same time we live in the great "we" of the Church, where the Word of God is alive. Moreover, other points are associated with it: listening to friends, listening to the priests who guide us, listening to the voice of today's Church; hence, listening to the voice of the events of this time and of creation that become decipherable in this profound context.

To sum up, therefore, I would say that God speaks to us in many ways. It is important to be in the "we" of the Church, in the "we" of the life of the Liturgy. It is important that I personalize this "we" in myself; it is important to be attentive to the other voices of the Lord, also letting ourselves be guided by the people who have experience of God, so to speak, and help us on this journey, so that this "we" becomes my "we," and I become one who truly belongs to this "we."

Thus, discernment grows, and personal friendship with God grows, the capacity to distinguish God's voice among the thousands of voices of today, which is always present and always speaks with us.

Claudio Fabbri, Diocese of Rome (Second-Year Philosophy):

Holy Father, how was the period of your formation to the priesthood organized? What interests did you cultivate? Considering the experience you have had, what are the cardinal points of priestly formation? In particular, what place does Mary occupy in it?

Pope Benedict XVI:

I think that our life at our seminary in Freising was organized in a very similar way to yours, even if I do not know your exact daily schedule. I think the day began at 6:30 or 7:00 A.M. with a half hour's meditation, when each one spoke silently with the Lord, trying to prepare his soul for the Sacred Liturgy. Holy Mass followed, breakfast, and then the morning lessons.

In the afternoon, seminars, study time, and then again common prayer. In the evening, the so-called *"puncta,"* which is when the spiritual director or rector of the seminary spoke to us on various evenings to help us discover the path of meditation; they did not give us a meditation composed in advance, but elements that might help each one of us personalize the Word of the Lord that was to be the object of our meditation.

This was the daily itinerary; then, naturally, there were the great feast days with a beautiful liturgy, music. . . . But it seems to me, and perhaps I will return to this at the end, that it is very important to have a discipline that precedes me and not to have to decide again, every day, what to do and how to live. There is a rule, a set discipline that waits for me and helps me live this in an orderly way.

Now, as to my preferences, naturally I followed the lessons with attention, as best I could. Initially, in the first two years of philosophy, it was above all the figure of St. Augustine who fascinated me from the very start, then also the Augustinian current in the Middle Ages: St. Bonaventure, the great Franciscans, the figure of St. Francis of Assisi.

Above all, I found St. Augustine's great humanity fascinating, because from the outset as a catechumen he was simply unable to identify with the Church, but instead had to have a spiritual struggle to find, little by little, access to the Word of God, to life with God, until he said his great "yes" to his Church.

This journey is so human. In it, we can also today see how one begins to enter into contact with God, how all the forms of our natural resistance must be taken seriously and then channeled to arrive at the great "yes" to the Lord. Thus, his theology conquered me in a very personal way, developed above all by preaching.

This is important because at the outset Augustine wanted to live a purely contemplative life, to write more books on philosophy ... but the Lord did not want him to, he made Augustine a priest and Bishop and so for the rest of his life, his work developed essentially in dialogue with a very simple people.

Moreover, he must have always personally discovered the meaning of the Scriptures, and likewise, must have taken this people's ability, their life context, into account to arrive at a realistic and at the same time very profound Christianity.

Then, naturally, for me exegesis was very important: we had two somewhat liberal but nevertheless great exegetes, also true believers, who fascinated us. I can say that Sacred Scripture really was the soul of our theological studies: we truly lived with Sacred Scripture and learned to love it, to converse with it.

I have already spoken of Patristics, of the encounter with the Fathers. Our dogmatics professor was also a very famous person and had nourished his dogmatics with the Fathers and with the Liturgy.

In his opinion, our liturgical formation was a very central point: there were still no liturgical faculties at that time, but our professor of pastoral studies gave us great courses in liturgy, and at the time he was also Rector of the seminary, so the liturgy was lived and celebrated, and thus liturgy taught and thought went together. These, together with Sacred Scripture, were the crucial points of our theological formation. I am always thankful to the Lord for this, because together they truly are the center of a priestly life.

Another interest was literature: it was obligatory to read Dostoevsky, it was fashionable at that time; then there were also the great French writers: Claudel, Mauriac, Bernanos; and also German literature. Furthermore, there was a German edition of Manzoni: at that time I did not speak Italian. So it was that in this sense we gave some sort of form to our human horizon.

Another great love was music, as well as the natural beauty of our land. With these preferences, these realities, I forged ahead on a journey that was not always easy. The Lord helped me to arrive as far as the "yes" of the priesthood, a "yes" that has accompanied me every day of my life.

Gianpiero Savino, Diocese of Taranto (First-Year Theology):

In the eyes of most people we might appear as young men who say their "yes" firmly and courageously and leave everything to follow the Lord; but we know that we are far from being truly consistent with that "yes." Trusting as sons, we confess to you the partiality of our response to Jesus' call and the daily effort of living a vocation that we feel is propelling us along the path of the definitive and the total. How can we respond to such a demanding vocation as that of shepherds of God's holy People while being constantly aware of our weakness and inconsistencies?

Benedict XVI:

It is good to recognize one's weakness because in this way we know that we stand in need of the Lord's grace. The Lord comforts us. In the Apostolic College there was not only Judas but also the good Apostles; yet, Peter fell, and many times the Lord reprimanded the Apostles for their slowness, the closure of their hearts, and their scant faith. He therefore simply shows us that none of us is equal to this great yes, equal to celebrating "in persona Christi," to living coherently in this context, to being united to Christ in his priestly mission.

To console us, the Lord has also given us these parables of the net with the good fish and the bad fish, of the field where wheat but also tares grow. He makes us realize that he came precisely to help us in our weakness and that he did not come, as he says, to call the just, those who claim they are righteous through and through and are not in need of grace, those who pray praising themselves; but he came to call those who know they are lacking, to provoke those who know they need the

Lord's forgiveness every day, that they need his grace in order to progress.

I think this is very important: to recognize that we need an ongoing conversion, that we are simply not there yet. St. Augustine, at the moment of his conversion, thought he had reached the heights of life with God, of the beauty of the sun that is his Word. He then had to understand that the journey after conversion is still a journey of conversion, that it remains a journey where the broad perspectives, joys, and lights of the Lord are not absent; nor are dark valleys absent through which we must wend our way with trust, relying on the goodness of the Lord.

Therefore, also the Sacrament of Reconciliation is important. It is not correct to think we must live like this, so that we are never in need of pardon. We must accept our frailty but keep on going, not giving up but moving forward and becoming converted ever anew through the Sacrament of Reconciliation for a new start, and thus grow and mature in the Lord by our communion with him.

It is also important of course not to isolate oneself, not to believe one is capable of going ahead alone. We truly need the company of priest friends and also lay friends who accompany and help us. It is very important for a priest, in the parish itself, to see how people trust in him and to experience, in addition to their trust, also their generosity in pardoning his weaknesses. True friends challenge us and help us to be faithful on our journey. It seems to me that this attitude of patience and humility can help us to be kind to others, to understand the weaknesses of others, and also help them to forgive as we forgive.

I think I am not being indiscreet if I say that today I received a beautiful letter from Cardinal Martini: I had congratulated him on his eightieth birthday—we are the same age; in thanking me he wrote, "I thank the Lord above all for the gift of perseverance. Today," he writes, "good is done rather *ad tempus, ad experimentum.* Good, in accordance with its essence, can only be done definitively; but to do it definitively we need the grace of perseverance. I pray each day," he concluded, "that the Lord will grant me this grace."

I return to St. Augustine: at first he was content with the grace of conversion; then he discovered the need for another grace, the grace of perseverance, one that we must ask the Lord for each day; but since—I return to what Cardinal Martini said—"the Lord has given me the grace of perseverance until now, I hope he will also give it to me in the last stage of my journey on this earth."

It seems to me that we must have trust in this gift of perseverance, but we must also pray to the Lord with tenacity, humility, and patience to help and sustain us with the gift of true "definitiveness" and to accompany us day after day to the very end, even if our way must pass through dark valleys. The gift of perseverance gives us joy, it gives us the certainty that we are loved by the Lord, and this love sustains us, helps us, and does not abandon us in our weakness.

Koicio Dimov, Diocese of Nicopolis, Bulgaria
(Second-Year Theology):

Most Blessed Father, commenting on the Way of the Cross in 2005, you spoke of the dirt in the Church; and in the Homily for the ordination of the Roman priests last year, you warned us of the risk "of careerism, the attempt to get to the top, to obtain a position through the Church." How do we face these problems as serenely and responsibly as possible?

Benedict XVI:

It is not an easy question, but it seems to me that I have already said, and it is an important point, that the Lord knows, knew from the beginning, that there is also sin in the Church, and for our humility it is important to recognize this and to see sin not only in others, in structures, in lofty hierarchical duties, but also in ourselves, to be in this way more humble and to learn that what counts before the Lord is not an ecclesial position, but what counts is to be in his love and to make his love shine forth.

Personally I consider St. Ignatius's prayer on this point to be very important. It says, "*Suscipe, Domine, universam meam libertatem; accipe memoriam, intellectum atque voluntatem omnem; quidquid habeo vel possideo mihi largitus es; id tibi totum restitoì ac tuae prorsus voluntati traoi gubernandum; amorem tuum cum gratia tua mihi dones ed dives sum satis, nec aliud quidquam ultra posco.*"[11]

Precisely this last part seems to me to be very important: to understand that the true treasure of our life is living in the Lord's love and never losing this love. Then we are really rich. A man who has discovered a great love feels really rich and knows that this is the true pearl, that this is the treasure of his life and not all the other things he may possess.

We have found, indeed, we have been found by the love of

---

11. Ignatius of Loyola, *Spiritual Exercises*, trans. Anthony Mottola (New York: Doubleday, 1989), 60.

the Lord, and the more we let ourselves be moved by his love in sacramental life, in prayer life, in the life of work, in our free time, the better we will understand that indeed, I have found the true pearl, all the rest is worthless, all the rest is important only to the extent that the Lord's love attributes these things to me. I am rich, I am truly rich and borne aloft if I am in this love. Here I find the center of life, its riches. Then let us allow ourselves to be guided, let us allow Providence to decide what to do with us.

Here a little story springs to my mind about St. Bakhita, the beautiful African Saint who was a slave in Sudan and then discovered the faith in Italy, who became a Sister. When she was old, the Bishop who was paying a visit to her religious house had not met her. He spotted this small, bent African Sister and said to Bakhita, "But what do you do, Sister?" and Sr. Bakhita replied, "I do the same as you, Your Excellency." Astonished, the Bishop asked her, "But what?," and Bakhita answered, "But Your Excellency, we both want to do the same thing: God's will."

This seems to me to be a most beautiful answer, the Bishop and the tiny Sister who was almost no longer capable of working, who were both doing the same thing in their different offices; they were seeking to do God's will and so were in the right place.

I also remember something St. Augustine said: All of us are always only disciples of Christ, and his throne is loftier, for his throne is the Cross, and only this height is the true height, communion with the Lord, also in his Passion. It seems to me, if we begin to understand this by a life of daily prayer, by a life of dedicated service to the Lord, we can free ourselves of these very human temptations.

195

Francesco Annesi, Diocese of Rome (Third-Year Theology):

Your Holiness, John Paul II's Apostolic Letter *Salvifici Doloris* makes it clear that suffering is a source of spiritual wealth for all who accept it in union with the sufferings of Christ. How can the priest today witness to the Christian meaning of suffering in a world that resorts to every legal or illegal means to eliminate any form of pain, and how should he behave toward those who are suffering without running the risk of being rhetorical or pathetic?

Benedict XVI:

Yes, what is he to do? Well, I think we should recognize that it is right to do our utmost to overcome the suffering of humanity and to help those suffering—there are so many of them in the world—to find a good life and to be relieved from the evils that we ourselves often cause: hunger, epidemics, etc.

However, at the same time, recognizing this duty to alleviate the suffering we ourselves have caused, we must also recognize and understand that suffering is an essential part of our human development.

I am thinking of the Lord's parable of the grain of wheat that fell to the ground and only in this way, by dying, could it bear fruit; and this falling to the ground and dying is not a momentary event but precisely a life process: to fall like a seed into the earth and thus to die, being transformed, being instruments of God so as to bear fruit.

It was not by chance that the Lord told his disciples: the Son of Man must go to Jerusalem to suffer; therefore, anyone who wants to be a disciple of mine must shoulder his cross so he can follow me. In fact, we are always somewhat similar to Peter, who said to the Lord, "No, Lord, this cannot happen to you, you must not suffer." We do not want to carry the Cross, we want to create a kingdom that is more human, more beautiful, on this earth.

This is totally mistaken: the Lord teaches it. However, Peter needed a lot of time, perhaps his entire life, in order to understand it; why is there this legend of the *Quo Vadis*? There is something true in it: learning that it is precisely in walking with the Lord's Cross that the journey will bear fruit. Thus, I would say that before talking to others, we ourselves must understand the mystery of the Cross.

Of course, Christianity gives us joy, for love gives joy. But love is also always a process of losing oneself, hence, a process of coming out of oneself; in this regard, it is also a painful process. Only in this way is it beautiful and helps us to mature and to attain true joy.

Anyone who seeks to affirm or to promise a life that is only happy and easy is a liar, because this is not the truth about man; the result is that one then has to flee to false paradises. And in this way one does not attain joy but self-destruction. Christianity proclaims joy to us, indeed; this joy, however, only develops on the path of love, and this path of love has to do with the Cross, with communion with the Crucified Christ. And it is presented through the grain of wheat that fell to the ground. When we begin to understand and accept this—every day, because every day brings some disappointment or other, some burden that may also cause pain—, when we accept this lesson of following Christ, just as the Apostles had to learn at this school, so we too will become capable of helping the suffering.

It is true that it is always difficult, if one who is more or less healthy and in good condition is obliged to comfort someone afflicted by a great evil, whether illness or the loss of love. In the face of these evils with which we are all familiar, everything appears almost inevitably rhetorical and pathetic.

Yet, I would say, if these people feel that we are "compassionate," that we want to share in carrying the Cross with them in communion with Christ, above all by praying with them, helping them with a silence full of sympathy, love, helping them as best we can, then can we become credible.

We must accept this, as perhaps at first our words appear purely words. However, if we really live in this spirit of truly following Jesus, we also find the way to be close with our sympathy.

Etymologically, sympathy means "com-passion" for the human being, helping him, praying, and thereby creating trust in the Lord's goodness that also exists in the darkest valley. Thus, we can open our hearts to the Gospel of Christ himself, who is the true Consoler; opening our hearts to the Holy Spirit, who is called the other Consoler, the other Paraclete, who is there, who is present.

We can open our hearts not because of our words, but because of the important teaching of Christ, his being with us, and thereby help make suffering and pain truly a grace of maturation, of communion with the Crucified and Risen Christ.

Marco Ceccarelli: Diocese of Rome, (Deacon):

Your Holiness, in the coming months my companions and I will be ordained priests. We will move from a well-regulated seminary life to the broader context of parish life. What advice can you give us to enable us to adjust as well as possible at the beginning of our priestly ministry?

Benedict XVI:

Well, here at the seminary you do have a very good routine. I would say as the first point that it is also important in the life of pastors of the Church, in the daily life of the priest, to preserve as far as possible a certain order. You should never skip Mass—a day without the Eucharist is incomplete—and thus already at the seminary we grow up with this daily liturgy. It seems to me very important that we feel the need to be with the Lord in the Eucharist, not as a professional obligation but truly as an interiorly felt duty, so that the Eucharist should never be missed.

Another important point is to make time for the Liturgy of the Hours and therefore, for this inner freedom: with all the burdens that exist, it frees us and helps us to be more open, to be deeply in touch with the Lord.

Of course, we must do all that is required by pastoral life, by the life of a parochial vicar or of a parish priest or by another priestly office. However, I would say, never forget these fixed points, the Eucharist and the Liturgy of the Hours, so that you have a certain order in the daily routine. As I said at the outset, we learned not to have to plan the timetable ever anew; "*Serva ordinem et ordo servabit te.*"[12] These are true words.

Next, it is important not to neglect communion with other priests, with one's companions on the way, and not to lose

12. Ancient adage: "*Serva ordinem et ordo servabit te*" (preserve order and order will preserve you).

one's personal contact with the Word of God, meditation. How should this be done? I have a fairly simple recipe for it: combine the preparation of the Sunday homily with personal meditation to ensure that these words are not only spoken to others but are really words said by the Lord to me myself, and developed in a personal conversation with the Lord.

For this to be possible, my advice is to begin early on Monday, for if one begins on Saturday it is too late, the preparation is hurried, and perhaps inspiration is lacking, for one has other things on one's mind. Therefore, I would say, already on Monday, simply read the Readings for the coming Sunday that perhaps seem very difficult: a little like those rocks at Massah and Meribah, where Moses said, "But how can water come from these rocks?"

Then stop thinking about these Readings and allow the heart to digest them. Words are processed in the unconscious, and return a little more every day. Obviously, books should also be consulted, as far as possible. And with this interior process, day by day, one sees that a response gradually develops. These words gradually unfold, they become words for me. And since I am a contemporary, they also become words for others. I can then begin to express what I perhaps see in my own theological language in the language of others; the fundamental thought, however, remains the same for others and for myself.

Thus, it is possible to have a lasting and silent encounter with the Word that does not demand a lot of time, which perhaps we do not have. But save a little time: only in this way does a Sunday homily mature for others, but my own heart is also touched by the Lord's Word. I am also in touch with a situation when perhaps I have little time available.

I would not dare now to offer too much advice, because life in the large city of Rome is a little different to what I experienced fifty-five years ago in our Bavaria. But I think these things are essential: the Eucharist, the Office of Readings, prayer, and a conversation every day, even a brief one, with the Lord on his words that I must proclaim. And never lose either your friendship with priests, listening to the voice of the living Church, or naturally, availability to the people entrusted to me, because from these very people, with their suffering, their faith experiences, their doubts and difficulties, we too can learn, seek and find God, find our Lord Jesus Christ.

29. Detachment and Communion

From *Homily of His Holiness During the Celebration of the First Vespers*, Roman Major Seminary, February 1, 2008

We are gathered together for first solemn Vespers of this Marian Feast that is so dear to you. We have listened to some verses from St. Paul's Letter to the Galatians in which he uses the expression "fullness of time" (cf. Gal 4:4). God alone can "fill the time" and make us experience the full meaning of our existence. God filled time with himself by sending his Only-Begotten Son, and in him he has made us his adoptive sons: sons in the Son. In Jesus and with Jesus, "the Way, and the Truth, and the Life" (Jn 14:6), we are now able to find exhaustive answers to the heart's deepest expectations. Once fear has been dispelled, trust in God, whom we even dare to call *"Abba! Father!"* (cf. Gal 4: 6), grows within us.

Dear seminarians, it is precisely because the gift of being adoptive sons of God had illuminated your lives that you were stirred by the desire to make others share in it too. This is why you are here, to develop your filial vocation and prepare yourselves for your future mission as apostles of Christ. It concerns a unified growth that, while permitting you to savor the joy of life with God the Father, it makes you feel so much more the urgent need to become messengers of the Gospel of his Son Jesus. It is the Holy Spirit who makes you attentive to this profound reality and makes you love it. All this cannot fail to kindle immense trust in you, for the gift you have received is amazing, it fills you with wonder and profound joy. You can therefore understand the role that Mary also has in your lives, invoked in your Seminary by the beautiful title, "Our Lady of Trust." Like the "Son, born of woman" (cf. Gal 4:4), of Mary, Mother of God, so your being sons of God means that you have her as Mother, as a true Mother.

Dear parents, you are probably the most surprised of all at what is happening in your sons. You probably imagined a different career for them than the mission for which they are now preparing. Who knows how often you find yourselves thinking about them: you think back to when they were children, then boys; to the times when they showed the first signs of their vocation or, in some cases on the contrary, to the years in which your son's life seemed remote from the Church. What happened? What meetings influenced their decisions? What inner enlightenment guided their footsteps? How could they then give up even promising prospects of life in order to choose to enter the Seminary? Let us look to Mary! The Gospel gives us to understand that she also asked herself many questions about her Son Jesus and pondered on him at length (cf. Lk 2:19, 51).

It is inevitable that in a certain manner, the vocations of children become the vocations of their parents, too. In seeking to understand your children and following them on their way, you too, dear fathers and dear mothers, very often find yourselves involved in a journey in which your faith is strengthened and renewed. You find yourselves sharing in the marvelous adventure of your sons. Indeed, even though it may seem that the priest's life does not attract most people's interest, it is in fact the most interesting and necessary adventure for the world, the adventure of showing, of making present, the fullness of life to which we all aspire. It is a very demanding adventure; and it could not be otherwise, since the priest is called to imitate Jesus, who "came not to be served but to serve, and to give his life as a ransom for many" (Mt 20:28).

Dear seminarians, these years of formation constitute an important time in which to prepare yourselves for the exalting mission to which the Lord calls you. Allow me to underline two aspects that mark your current experience. First of all, your seminary years involve a certain detachment from ordinary life, a certain "wilderness," so that the Lord can speak to your heart (cf. Hos 2:14). Indeed, his voice is not loud but rather subdued, it is "a still small voice" (1 Kgs 19:12). Thus, if the Lord's voice is to be heard, an atmosphere of silence is essential. For this reason the Seminary offers space and times for daily prayer; it takes great care of the liturgy, meditation on the Word of God, and Eucharistic adoration. At the same time, it demands that you devote long hours to study: in praying and studying you can build within yourselves the man of God whom you must be and whom people expect a priest to be.

Then there is a second aspect of your life: during your seminary years, you live together; your formation for the priesthood also involves this community aspect that is of great importance. In following Jesus, the Apostles were formed together. Your communion is not limited to the present time but also concerns the future: the pastoral action that awaits you must see you joining forces, as though in one body, in one *ordo*, that of priests who, together with the Bishop, care for the Christian community. May you love this "family life" that is an anticipation for you of that "sacramental brotherhood" that must characterize every diocesan priest.[13]

All this reminds you that God calls you to be holy, that holiness is the secret of the true success of your priestly ministry. From this moment holiness must be the goal of your every choice and decision. Entrust this desire and this daily commitment to Mary, Mother of Trust! This most pacifying title corresponds to the invitation, repeated in the Gospel and addressed to the Virgin by the Angel and then so many other times by Jesus to his disciples: "Do not be afraid" (cf. Lk 1:30). "Do not be afraid, for I am with you," says the Lord. In the icon of Our Lady of Trust, in which the Child points to the Mother, it seems that Jesus is adding, "Look at your Mother and do not fear." Dear seminarians, follow the Seminary curriculum with your minds open to truth, transparency, and dialogue with those who guide you. This will enable you to respond in a very simple and hum-

13. Cf. Second Vatican Council, Decree *Presbyterorum Ordinis* (December 7, 1965), no. 8.

ble way to the One who calls you, freeing yourselves from the risk of creating a strictly personal project. Dear parents and friends, accompany the seminarians with prayer and with your constant material and spiritual support. I also assure you all of my remembrance in prayer, as I joyfully impart the Apostolic Blessing to you.

30. *Theological Formation*

From *Address of His Holiness Benedict XVI,* Meeting with Priests, Seminarians, and Students of the Pontifical Theological Faculty of Sardinia, September 7, 2008

In my mind's eye, I keep alive an evocative image of this morning's Solemn Eucharistic celebration at the Basilica of Our Lady of Bonaria. Near Mary, special Patroness of all of Sardinia, an appointment was made for the parochial communities of the entire region. And now, almost as a prolongation of that spiritual encounter, I have the joy of meeting with you, dear priests, seminarians, students, and teachers of the Pontifical Theological Faculty of Sardinia, in this Cathedral, it too dedicated to the holy Virgin Mary. In this ancient temple, renovated and embellished over the course of the years by the care of zealous Pastors, everything speaks of faith: a living faith, witnessed to by the devout safeguarding of the relics of the Martyrs of Cagliari, among which I am happy to note are the Saint Bishops Siricius, Martin, Ninian, Hillary, Fabricius, and Juvenal.

I wholeheartedly thank Archbishop Giuseppe Mani for the renewed greeting that he has addressed to me in the name of all the Bishops and priests of Cagliari and of the region. Meeting with you, dear priests here present, I think with affection and gratitude of your brethren who work on the Island, on a terrain ploughed and cultivated with apostolic ardor by those who have preceded you. Yes! Sardinia has known priests who, as authentic teachers of the faith, have left wonderful examples of loyalty to Christ and to the Church. The same inestimable treasure of faith, of spirituality, and of culture is entrusted to you today. It is placed in your hands so that you may be attentive and wise administrators of it. Take care of it and guard it with Evangelical joy and passion!

Now I affectionately address the community of seminarians and of the Theological Faculty, where many of you have been able to carry out doctrinal and pastoral formation, and where currently many young people go to prepare for their future ministerial priesthood. I am anxious to thank the teachers and professors who dedicate themselves daily to such an important apostolic work. To accompany candidates for the priestly mission on their formative journey means above all to help them conform themselves to Christ. In this duty, you, dear educators and professors, are called to play an irreplaceable role, since it is truly during these years that one lays the foundations of their future priestly ministry. This is why, as on different occasions I have been able to emphasize, it is necessary to guide seminarians to a personal experience of God through personal and communal daily prayer, and above all through the Eucharist, celebrated and experienced as the center of their very existence. In the Post-Synodal Exhortation *Pastores Dabo Vobis* John Paul II wrote, "Intellectual formation in theology and formation in the spiritual life, in particular the life of prayer, meet and strength-

THE MEANING OF SEMINARY FORMATION

en each other, without detracting in any way from the sound-
ness of research or from the spiritual tenor of prayer."[14]

Dear seminarians and students of the Theological Faculty,
you know that theological formation—as my Venerable Predecessor recalled further in the cited Apostolic Exhortation—is
very complex and demanding work. It must lead you to possess a "complete and unified" vision of revealed truths and of
their acceptance into the faith experience of the Church. From
this pours forth the double demand of knowing the entirety of
Christian truth and knowing those truths not as truths separated one from the other, but in an organic way, as a union, as the
one truth of faith in God, building "a synthesis which will be
the result of the contributions of the different theological disciplines, the specific nature of which acquires genuine value only
in their profound coordination."[15] This [synthesis] demonstrates
to us the unity of truth, the unity of our faith. Besides, in these
years, each activity and initiative must dispose you to administer the charity of Christ the Good Shepherd. To him you are
called to be tomorrow's ministers and witnesses: ministers of
his grace and witnesses of his love. Next to study and pastoral
and apostolic experience from which you can draw, do not forget, however, to put the constant quest for intimate communion
with Christ in the first place. Here, only here, rests the secret of
your true apostolic success.

Dear priests, dear aspirants to the priesthood and to consecrated life, God wants you for himself and calls you to be

14. Cf. Pope John Paul II, Apostolic Exhortation *Pastores Dabo Vobis*, no. 53.
15. Ibid., no. 54.

workers in his vineyard, just as he did many men and women throughout the Christian history of your beautiful Island. They knew to respond with a generous "yes" to his call. I am thinking of, for example, the evangelizing work carried out by the religious: from the Franciscan to the Mercedarians, from the Dominicans to the Jesuits, from the Benedictines to the Vincentians, from the Salesians to the Piarists, from the Christian School Brothers to the Josephine Fathers, to the Orioni Fathers and so many others still. And how could the great flowering of female religious vocations, for which Sardinia has been a true and proper garden, be forgotten? In many Orders and Congregations Sardinian women are present, especially in cloistered monasteries. Without this great "cloud of witnesses," (cf. Heb 12:1) it certainly would have been much more difficult to spread the love of Christ in the towns, families, schools, hospitals, prisons, and workplaces. What a heritage of good has come, accumulating grace by their dedication! Without the seed of Christianity Sardinia would be more fragile and poor. Together with you I thank God who never lets the witnesses of saints fail to guide his people!

Dear brothers and sisters, it is now up to you to carry on the work of good accomplished by those who have gone before you. To you, in particular, dear priests—and I address with affection all the priests of Sardinia—I assure my spiritual nearness, so that you may respond to the Lord's call with total loyalty as, even recently, some of your brothers have done. I recall Fr. Graziano Muntoni, a priest of the Diocese of Nuoro, killed on Christmas Eve of 1998, while he was going to celebrate Mass, and Fr. Battore Carzedda of the P.I.M.E., who gave his life so that believers of all religions would open to sincere dialogue sustained by love. Do not be frightened, do not be discouraged by difficulties: the grain and the weeds, as we know, will grow together until the end of the world (cf. Mt 13:30). It is important to be seeds of good grain that, fallen to earth, bear fruit. Deepen the awareness of your identity: the priest, for the Church and in the Church, is a humble but real sign of the one, eternal Priest who is Jesus. He must proclaim his word authoritatively, renew his acts of pardon and offering, and exercise loving concern in the service of his flock, in communion with the Pastors and faithfully docile to the teaching of the Magisterium. Therefore, rekindle the charism you have received with the imposition of hands (cf. 2 Tm 1:6) each day, identifying with Jesus Christ in his triple function of sanctifying, teaching, and shepherding the flock. May Mary Most Holy, Mother of the Church, protect you and accompany you. On my behalf I bless all of you, with a special remembrance for the elderly and sick priests, and for all the people entrusted to your pastoral care.

31. *A Personal Relationship with Christ*

From *Address of His Holiness Benedict XVI to the Communities of the Pontifical Regional Seminaries of Marche*, Puglia, Abruzzo e Molise, November 29, 2008

I am particularly pleased to welcome you on the occasion of the centenary of the foundation of your respective Regional Seminaries, which were established as a result of the encouragement of Pope St. Pius X, who urged the Italian Bishops, especially those of the central and southern part of the Peninsula, to consider congregating Seminaries in order to provide more effectively for the formation of candidates to the priesthood. I greet you all with affection, starting with Archbishops Edoardo Menichelli, Carlo Ghidelli, and Francesco Cacucci, whom I thank for the words with which they have interpreted your common sentiments. I greet the rectors, the formation staff, the professors, and the students and all who live and work daily in your institutions. On this important occasion, I would like to join you in praising the Lord, who in this century has accompanied with his grace the lives of many priests who have trained at these important educational institutions. Many of them are involved today in the various sectors of your local Churches, in the mission *ad gentes*, and in other services to the universal Church; some have been called to hold offices that entail great ecclesial responsibility.

I would now like to address you in particular, dear Seminarians, who are preparing to be workers in the Lord's vineyard. As the recent Assembly of the Synod of Bishops recalled, among the prioritized tasks of the presbyterate is that of scattering the Word of God in the field of the world in large handfuls. Like the seed in the Gospel parable, it actually seems very small, but once it has sprouted it grows into a great shrub and bears abundant fruit (cf. Mt 13:31–32). The Word of God that you will be called to sow in large handfuls and that bears within it eternal life is Christ himself, the only one who can change the human heart and renew the world. But we might well ask ourselves: does contemporary man still feel the need for Christ and for his message of salvation?

In today's social context a certain culture seems to be showing us the face of a self-sufficient humanity desirous of accomplishing its own projects by itself, which chooses to be the sole author of its own destiny and consequently considers that God's presence is irrelevant; it therefore excludes him de facto from its choices and decisions. In a climate at times marked by a rationalism closed in on itself, which considers the practical sciences the only form of knowledge, the rest becomes completely subjective, and consequently the religious experience also risks being perceived as a subjective choice, neither essential nor crucial for life. Today, of course, for these and other reasons, it has certainly become more difficult to believe, always more difficult to accept the Truth that is Christ, always more difficult to spend one's life for the cause of the Gospel. However, as the news reports daily, contemporary man often seems lost and worried about his future, in search of certainties and longing for reliable reference points. Moreover, as in every epoch, people in the third millennium need God and sometimes seek him even without realizing it. The task of Christians, and especially of priests, is to take in this deep yearning of the human heart and to offer to all, with the means and in the manner required by the needs of the times, the unchanging and therefore always alive and actual Word of eternal life that is Christ, Hope of the world.

With a view to this important mission that you will be called to carry out in the Church, the seminary years assume great value. This is a period designed for formation and discernment; years in which priority must be the constant pursuit of a personal relationship with Jesus, an intimate experience of his love that is acquired first of all through prayer and through contact with the Sacred Scriptures, read, interpreted, and meditated upon in the faith of the ecclesial community. In this Pauline Year, how can I fail to propose the Apostle Paul to you as a model to inspire you in your preparation for the apostolic ministry? His extraordinary experience on the road to Damascus transformed him from a persecutor of Christians to a witness of the Lord's Resurrection, ready to lay down his life for the Gospel. He had been a faithful observer of all the prescriptions of the Torah and the Jewish traditions, but after his encounter with Jesus, he writes in his Letter to the Philippians, "whatever gain I had, I counted as loss for the sake of Christ" (Phil 3:7). "For his sake," he added, "I have suffered the loss of all things, and count them as refuse, in order that I may gain Christ and be found in him" (cf. Phil 3:7–9). Conversion did not eliminate what was good and true in his life but permitted him to interpret the wisdom and truth of the law and of the prophets in a new way and thus be enabled to converse with all, after the example of the divine Teacher.

In imitation of St. Paul, dear Seminarians, never tire of encountering Christ in listening, in reading and in studying Sacred Scripture, in prayer and in personal meditation, in the liturgy and in every other daily activity. Your role is important in this regard, dear formators, called to be witnesses for your pupils, even before being teachers of evangelical life. Because of their own typical characteristics, Regional Seminaries can be privileged places for the formation of seminarians in diocesan spirituality, engraving this formation in the broader ecclesial and regional context with wisdom and balance. May your institutions also be "homes" that welcome vocations in order to impress an even greater impetus upon vocations ministry, taking special care of the world of youth and teaching them the great evangelical and missionary ideals.

Dear friends, as I thank you for your visit, I invoke upon each one of you the motherly protection of the Virgin Mother of Christ, whom the Advent liturgy presents to us as the model of one who watches while awaiting the glorious return of her divine Son. I confidently entrust you to her. Have frequent recourse to her intercession so that she may help you to keep alert and watchful. For my part, I assure you of my affection and my daily prayers, while I warmly bless you all.

32. A Demanding Path

From *Address of His Holiness Benedict XVI to the Community of the French Seminary in Rome*, June 6, 2009

I welcome you with joy on the occasion of the celebrations of these days, which mark an important moment in the history of the Pontifical French Seminary in Rome. After a century and a half of faithful service, the Congregation of the Holy Spirit, which had been in charge of conducting the Seminary since its foundation, has now handed it over to the Bishops' Conference of France.

We must thank the Lord for the work carried out in this institution where, since it opened, almost five thousand seminarians or young priests have been trained for their future vocation. In acknowledging the work of the members of the Congregation of the Holy Spirit, Fathers and Brothers, I would like to entrust to the Lord in particular the apostolates that the Congregation founded by Venerable Fr. Libermann preserves and develops across the world, and most especially in Africa, based on his charism, which has lost none of its power and justice. May the Lord bless the Congregation and its missions.

The task of forming priests is a delicate mission. The formation offered by the Seminary is demanding, because a portion of the People of God will be entrusted to the pastoral solicitude of the future priests, the People that Christ saved and for whom he gave his life. It is right for seminarians to remember that if the Church demands much of them it is because they are to care for those whom Christ ransomed at such a high price. Many qualities are required of future priests: human maturity, spiritual qualities, apostolic zeal, intellectual rigor.... To achieve these virtues, candidates to the priesthood must not only be able to witness to them to their formation teachers, but, even more, they must be the first to benefit from these same qualities lived and shared by those who are in charge of helping them to attain maturity. It is a law of our humanity and our faith that we are all too often capable of giving only what we ourselves have previously received from God through the ecclesial and human mediation that he has established. Those who are placed in charge of discernment and formation must remember that the hope they have for others is in the first place a duty for themselves.

This passing on of witnessing coincides with the beginning of the *Year for Priests*. This coincidence is a grace for the new team of priest-formation teachers gathered by the Bishops' Conference of France. While the team receives its mission, like the whole Church, it is given the possibility to examine more deeply the identity of the priest, a mystery of grace and mercy. I would like to mention here the eminent figure of Cardinal Suhard, who said of Christ's ministers, "Eternal paradox of the priest. He bears within him those who are contrary. He reconciles, at the price of his life, fidelity to God with fidelity to man. He seems poor and feeble.... He has neither political power nor financial means, nor the force of arms that others use to conquer the earth. His strength lies in being unarmed and being "able to do all things in the One who gives him strength."[16] May these words that so vividly evoke the figure of the Holy Curé d'Ars ring out as a vocational appeal to numerous young Christians in France who desire a useful and fruitful life in order to serve God's love.

The particular characteristic of the French Seminary is its location in the city of Peter, echoing the desire of Paul VI.[17] I hope that during their stay in Rome the seminarians will give priority to becoming acquainted with the Church's history in order to discover the breadth of her catholicity and her living unity around the Successor of Peter, and that love of the Church will thus be rooted in their hearts forever.

As I invoke upon you all the Lord's abundant graces through the intercession of the Blessed Virgin Mary, St. Clare, and Blessed Pius IX, I very warmly impart the Apostolic Blessing to all of you and to your families, to the former seminarians who have been unable to come here, and to all the Seminary's lay personnel.

16. Fulget *Ecclesia* (December 1960), no. 141:21.

17. Cf. Pope Paul VI, *Address to the Alumni of the French Pontifical Seminary*, September 12, 1968.

33. Saint John Eudes and the Formation
of the Diocesan Clergy

From *General Audience*, Wednesday, August 19, 2009

Today is the liturgical Memorial of St. John Eudes, a tireless apostle of the devotion to the Sacred Hearts of Jesus and Mary who lived in France in the seventeenth century, which was marked by opposing religious phenomena and serious political problems. It was the time of the Thirty Years' War, which devastated not only a large part of Central Europe but also souls. While contempt for the Christian faith was being spread by certain currents of thought that then prevailed, the Holy Spirit was inspiring a spiritual renewal full of fervor with important figures such as de Bérulle, St. Vincent de Paul, St. Louis-Marie Grignon de Montfort, and Saint John Eudes. This great "French school" of holiness also included St. John Mary Vianney. Through a mysterious design of Providence, my venerable Predecessor Pius XI canonized John Eudes and the Curé d'Ars together, on May 31, 1925, holding up to the whole world two extraordinary examples of priestly holiness.

In the context of the Year for Priests, I want to dwell on the apostolic zeal of St. John Eudes, which he focused in particular on the formation of the diocesan clergy. The saints are true interpreters of Sacred Scripture. In the experience of their lives the saints have verified the truth of the Gospel; thus they introduce us into a knowledge and understanding of the Gospel. In 1563 the Council of Trent issued norms for the establishment of diocesan seminaries and for the formation of priests, since the Council was well aware that the whole crisis of the Reformation was also conditioned by the inadequate formation of priests who were not properly prepared for the priesthood either intellectually or spiritually, in their hearts or in their minds. This was in 1563; but since the application and realization of the norms was delayed both in Germany and in France, St. John Eudes saw the consequences of this omission. Prompted by a lucid awareness of the grave need for spiritual assistance in which souls lay because of the inadequacy of the majority of the clergy, the Saint, who was a parish priest, founded a congregation specifically dedicated to the formation of priests. He founded his first seminary in the university town of Caen, a particularly appreciated experience that he very soon extended to other dioceses. The path of holiness, which he took himself and proposed to his followers, was founded on steadfast trust in the love that God had revealed to humanity in the priestly Heart of Christ and in the maternal Heart of Mary. In those times of cruelty, of the loss of interiority, he turned to the heart to speak to the heart, a saying of the Psalms very well interpreted by St. Augustine. He wanted to recall people, men and women and especially future priests, to the heart by showing them the priestly Heart of Christ and the motherly Heart of Mary. Every priest must be a witness and an apostle of this love for Christ's Heart and Mary's Heart. And here we come to our own time.

Today too people feel in need of priests who witness to God's infinite mercy with a life totally "conquered" by Christ and who learn to do this in the years of their seminary training. After the Synod in 1990 Pope John Paul II published the Apostolic Exhortation *Pastores Dabo Vobis* in which he returned to and updated the norms of the Council of Trent and stressed above all the necessary continuity between the priest's initial and continuing formation. For him this is a true starting point for an authentic reform of the life and apostolate of priests. It is also the key to preventing the "new evangelization" from being merely an attractive slogan and to ensuring that it is expressed in reality. The foundations laid in seminary formation constitute that indispensable *"humus spiritual"* in which "to learn Christ," letting oneself be gradually configured to him, the one and only High Priest and Good Shepherd. The seminary period should therefore be seen as the actualization of the moment when the Lord Jesus, after calling the Apostles and before sending them out to preach, asks them to be with him (cf. Mk 3:14). When St. Mark recounts the calling of the Twelve Apostles he says that Jesus had a twofold purpose: firstly that they should be with him, and secondly, that they should be sent out to preach. Yet, in being with him always, they really proclaim Christ and bring the reality of the Gospel to the world.

During this Year for Priests I ask you, dear brothers and sisters, to pray for priests and for all those who are preparing to receive the extraordinary gift of the ministerial priesthood. I address to you all and thus I conclude the exhortation of St. John Eudes, who said to priests, "Give yourselves to Jesus in order to enter the immensity of his great Heart which contains the Heart of his Holy Mother and the hearts of all the Saints and lose yourselves in this abyss of love, charity, mercy, humility, purity, patience, submission and holiness."[18] With this in mind, let us now sing the "Our Father" in Latin.

18. John Eudes, *The Admirable Heart of Mary*, trans. Charles di Targiani and Ruth Hauser (New York: P. J. Kennedy and Sons, 1948), 268.

34. *Witnessing Christ*

From *Message of the Holy Father for the 47th World Day
of Prayer for Vocations*, April 25, 2010

The 47th World Day of Prayer for Vocations, to be celebrated on the Fourth Sunday of Easter—Good Shepherd Sunday—April 25, 2010, gives me the opportunity to offer for your meditation a theme that is most fitting for this Year for Priests: *Witness Awakens Vocations*. The fruitfulness of our efforts to promote vocations depends primarily on God's free action, yet, as pastoral experience confirms, it is also helped by the quality and depth of the personal and communal witness of those who have already answered the Lord's call to the ministerial priesthood and to the consecrated life, for their witness is then able to awaken in others a desire to respond generously to Christ's call. This theme is thus closely linked to the life and mission of priests and of consecrated persons. Hence I wish to invite all those whom the Lord has called to work in his vineyard to renew their faithful response, particularly in this Year for Priests that I proclaimed on the 150th anniversary of the death of Saint John Mary Vianney, the Curé of Ars, an ever-timely model of a priest and a pastor.

In the Old Testament the prophets knew that they were called to witness by their own lives to the message they proclaimed and were prepared to face misunderstanding, rejection, and persecution. The task that God entrusted to them engaged them fully, like a "burning fire" in the heart, a fire that could not be contained (cf. Jer 20:9). As a result, they were prepared to hand over to the Lord not only their voice, but their whole existence. In the fullness of time, Jesus, sent by the Father (cf. Jn 5:36), would bear witness to the love of God for all human beings, without distinction, with particular attention to the least ones, sinners, the outcast, and the poor. Jesus is the supreme Witness to God and to his concern for the salvation of all. At the dawn of the new age, John the Baptist, by devoting his whole life to preparing the way for Christ, bore witness that the promises of God are fulfilled in the Son of Mary of Nazareth. When John saw Jesus coming to the river Jordan where he was baptizing, he pointed him out to his disciples as "the lamb of God, who takes away the sin of the world" (Jn 1:29). His testimony was so effective that two of his disciples, "hearing him say this, followed Jesus" (Jn 1:37).

Similarly the calling of Peter, as we read in the Evangelist John, occurred through the witness of his brother Andrew, who, after meeting the Master and accepting his invitation to stay with him, felt the need to share immediately with Peter what he discovered by "staying" with the Lord: "We have found the Messiah (which means Christ). He then brought him to Jesus" (Jn 1:41–42). This was also the case for Nathanael, Bartholomew, thanks to the witness of yet another disciple, Philip, who joyfully told him of his great discovery: "We have found him of whom Moses in the law and also the prophets wrote, Jesus of Nazareth, the son of Joseph" (Jn 1:45). God's free and gracious initiative encounters and challenges the human responsibility of all those who accept his invitation to become, through their own witness, the instruments of his divine call. This occurs in the Church even today: the Lord makes use of the witness of priests who are faithful to their mission in order to awaken new priestly and religious vocations for the service of the People of God. For this reason, I would like to mention three aspects of the life of a priest that I consider essential for an effective priestly witness.

A fundamental element, one that can be seen in every vocation to the priesthood and the consecrated life, is friendship with Christ. Jesus lived in constant union with the Father, and this is what made the disciples eager to have the same experience; from him they learned to live in communion and unceasing dialogue with God. If the priest is a "man of God," one who belongs to God and helps others to know and love him, he cannot fail to cultivate a deep intimacy with God, abiding in his love and making space to hear his Word. Prayer is the first form of witness that awakens vocations. Like the Apostle Andrew, who tells his brother that he has come to know the Master, so too anyone who wants to be a disciple and witness of Christ must have "seen" him personally, come to know him, and learned to love him and to abide with him.

Another aspect of the consecration belonging to the priesthood and the religious life is the complete gift of oneself to God. The Apostle John writes, "By this we know love, that he laid down his life for us; and therefore we ought to lay down our lives for the brethren" (1 Jn 3:16). With these words, he invites the disciples to enter into the very mind of Jesus who in his entire life did the will of the Father, even to the ultimate gift of himself on the Cross. Here, the mercy of God is shown in all its fullness; a merciful love that has overcome the darkness of evil, sin, and death. The figure of Jesus who, at the Last Supper, rises from the table, lays aside his garments, takes a towel, girds himself with it, and stoops to wash the feet of the Apostles, expresses the sense of service and gift manifested in his entire existence, in obedience to the will of the Father (cf. Jn 13:3–15). In following Jesus, everyone called to a life of special consecration must do his utmost to testify that he has given himself completely to God. This is the source of his ability to give himself in turn to those whom Providence entrusts to him in his pastoral ministry with complete, constant, and faithful devotion, and with the joy of becoming a companion on the journey to so many brothers and sisters, enabling them too to become open to meeting Christ, so that his Word may become a light to their footsteps. The story of every vocation is almost always intertwined with the testimony of a priest who joyfully lives the gift of himself to his brothers and sisters for the sake of the Kingdom of God. This is because the presence and words of a priest have the ability to raise questions and to lead even to definitive decisions.[19]

A third aspect that necessarily characterizes the priest and the consecrated person is a life of communion. Jesus showed that the mark of those who wish to be his disciples is profound communion in love: "By this all men will know that you are my disciples, if you have love for one another" (Jn 13:35). In a particular way the priest must be a man of communion, open to all, capable of gathering into one the pilgrim flock that the goodness of the Lord has entrusted to him, helping to overcome divisions, to heal rifts, to settle conflicts and misunderstandings, and to forgive offences. In July 2005, speaking to the clergy of Aosta, I noted that if young people see priests who appear dis-

19. Cf. Pope John Paul II, Apostolic Exhortation *Pastores Dabo Vobis*, no. 39.

tant and sad, they will hardly feel encouraged to follow their example. They will remain hesitant if they are led to think that this is the life of a priest. Instead, they need to see the example of a communion of life that can reveal to them the beauty of being a priest. Only then will a young man say, "Yes, this could be my future; I can live like this."[20] The Second Vatican Council, in speaking of the witness that awakens vocations, emphasizes the example of charity and of fraternal cooperation that priests must offer.[21]

Here I would like to recall the words of my venerable Predecessor John Paul II: "The very life of priests, their unconditional dedication to God's flock, their witness of loving service to the Lord and to his Church—a witness marked by free acceptance of the Cross in the spirit of hope and Easter joy—their fraternal unity and zeal for the evangelization of the world are the first and most convincing factor in the growth of vocations."[22] It can be said that priestly vocations are born of contact with priests, as a sort of precious legacy handed down by word, example, and a whole way of life.

The same can be said with regard to the consecrated life. The very life of men and women religious proclaims the love of Christ whenever they follow him in complete fidelity to the Gospel and joyfully make their own its criteria for judgment and conduct. They become "signs of contradiction" for the world, whose thinking is often inspired by materialism,

20. Pope Benedict XVI, *Meeting with Diocesan Clergy of Aosta*, Parish Church at Introd (Aosta Valley), July 25, 2005.

21. Cf. Second Vatican Council, Decree *Optatam Totius*, no. 2.

22. Cf. Pope John Paul II, Apostolic Exhortation *Pastores Dabo Vobis*, no. 41.

THE MEANING OF SEMINARY FORMATION

self-centeredness, and individualism. By letting themselves be won over by God through self-renunciation, their fidelity and the power of their witness constantly awaken in the hearts of many young people the desire to follow Christ in their turn, in a way that is generous and complete. To imitate Christ, chaste, poor, and obedient, and to identify with him: this is the ideal of the consecrated life, a witness to the absolute primacy of God in human life and history.

Every priest, every consecrated person, faithful to his or her vocation, radiates the joy of serving Christ and draws all Christians to respond to the universal call to holiness. Consequently, in order to foster vocations to the ministerial priesthood and the consecrated life, and to be more effective in promoting the discernment of vocations, we cannot do without the example of those who have already said "yes" to God and to his plan for the life of each individual. Personal witness, in the form of concrete existential choices, will encourage young people for their part to make demanding decisions affecting their future. Those who would assist them need to have the skills for encounter and dialogue that are capable of enlightening and accompanying them, above all through the example of life lived as a vocation. This was what the holy Curé of Ars did: always in close contact with his parishioners, he taught them "primarily by the witness of his life. It was from his example that the faithful learned to pray."[23]

May this World Day once again offer many young people a precious opportunity to reflect on their own vocation and to be faithful to it in simplicity, trust, and complete openness. May

23. Pope Benedict XVI, *Letter Proclaiming the Year for Priests* (June 16, 2009).

the Virgin Mary, Mother of the Church, watch over each tiny seed of a vocation in the hearts of those whom the Lord calls to follow him more closely, may she help it to grow into a mature tree, bearing much good fruit for the Church and for all humanity. With this prayer, to all of you I impart my Apostolic Blessing.

35. *Cultivate a Genuinely Catholic Culture*

From *Address of His Holiness Benedict XVI to the Pontifical North American College*, January 9, 2010

I am pleased to welcome the alumni of the Pontifical North American College, together with the Rector, faculty, and students of the seminary on the Janiculum Hill, and the student priests of the Casa Santa Maria dell'Umiltà. Our meeting comes at the conclusion of the celebrations marking the 150th anniversary of the College's establishment by my predecessor Blessed Pius IX. On this happy occasion I willingly join you in thanking the Lord for the many ways in which the College has remained faithful to its founding vision by training generations of worthy preachers of the Gospel and ministers of the sacraments, devoted to the Successor of Peter and committed to the building up of the Church in the United States of America.

It is appropriate, in this Year for Priests, that you have returned to the College and this Eternal City in order to give thanks for the academic and spiritual formation that has nourished your priestly ministry over the years. The present Reunion is an opportunity not only to remember with gratitude the time of your studies, but also to reaffirm your filial affection for the Church of Rome, to recall the apostolic labors of the countless alumni who have gone before you, and to recommit yourselves to the high ideals of holiness, fidelity, and pastoral zeal that you embraced on the day of your ordination. It is likewise an occasion to renew your love for the College and your appreciation of its distinctive mission to the Church in your country.

During my Pastoral Visit to the United States, I expressed my conviction that the Church in America is called to cultivate "an intellectual 'culture' which is genuinely Catholic, confident in the profound harmony of faith and reason, and prepared to bring the richness of faith's vision to bear on the pressing issues which affect the future of American society."[24] As Blessed Pius IX rightly foresaw, the Pontifical North American College in Rome is uniquely prepared to help meet this perennial challenge. In the century and a half since its foundation, the College has offered its students an exceptional experience of the universality of the Church, the breadth of her intellectual and spiritual tradition, and the urgency of her mandate to bring Christ's saving truth to the men and women of every time and place. I am confident that, by emphasizing these hallmarks of a Roman education in every aspect of its program of formation, the College will continue to produce wise and generous pastors capable of transmitting the Catholic faith in its integrity, bringing Christ's infinite mercy to the weak and the lost, and enabling America's Catholics to be a leaven of the Gospel in the social, political, and cultural life of their nation.

24. Pope Benedict XVI, *Homily at Nationals Stadium*, Apostolic Journey to the United States, Washington, D.C., April 17, 2008.

Dear brothers, I pray that in these days you will be renewed in the gift of the Holy Spirit that you received on the day of your ordination. In the College chapel, dedicated to the Blessed Virgin Mary under the title of the Immaculate Conception, Our Lady is portrayed in the company of four outstanding models and patrons of priestly life and ministry: Saint Gregory the Great, Saint Pius X, Saint John Mary Vianney, and Saint Vincent de Paul. During this Year for Priests, may these great saints continue to watch over the students who daily pray in their midst; may they guide and sustain your own ministry and intercede for the priests of the United States. With cordial good wishes for the spiritual fruitfulness of the coming days, and with great affection in the Lord, I impart to you my Apostolic Blessing, which I willingly extend to all the alumni and friends of the Pontifical North American College.

36. Our Fulfillment Is in Christ

From *Address of His Holiness Benedict XVI to the Community of the Pontifical Ethiopian College*, January 29, 2011

I am glad to welcome you on the happy occasion of the 150th anniversary of the birth in Heaven of St. Justin De Jacobis. I cordially greet each one of you, dear priests and seminarians of the Pontifical Ethiopian College, whom Divine Providence has brought to live beside the tomb of the Apostle Peter, a sign of the ancient and profound ties of communion that bind the Church that is in Ethiopia and in Eritrea with the Apostolic See.

I offer a special greeting to the Rector, Fr. Teclezghi Bahta, whom I thank for his courteous words introducing our meeting, explaining the various important circumstances that led to it. I welcome you today with special affection and, together with you, I am pleased to remember the communities you come from.

I would now like to reflect on the luminous figure of St. Justin De Jacobis, whose important anniversary you celebrated last July 31. A praiseworthy son of St. Vincent de Paul, St. Justin lived exemplarily, "making himself all things to all people," especially in service to the Abyssinian people. At the age of thirty-eight he was sent by Cardinal Franzoni, the then Prefect of Propaganda Fide, as a missionary to Tigrai, Ethiopia. He worked first in Adua and then in Guala, where he immediately thought of forming Ethiopian priests, and founded a seminary called "College of the Immaculate Virgin." In his zealous ministry he worked tirelessly to ensure that this portion of the People of God might rediscover the original fervor of faith, sown by the first evangelizer, St. Frumentius.[25] With farsightedness Justin perceived that attention to the cultural context must be a privileged path on which the Lord's grace would form new generations of Christians. Learning the local language and encouraging the age-old liturgical tradition of the Rite of those communities, his approach was effectively ecumenical. For more than twenty years his generous priestly, then episcopal ministry benefited all those he met and loved, as living members of the people entrusted to his care.

---

25. Cf. Rufinus of Aquileia, *Apologiae In Sanctum Hieronimum Libri Duo, Patrologia Cursus Completus*, Series Patrologia Latina, ed. Jacques P. Migne (Paris: 1844–64), 21:476–80.

Because of his enthusiasm for education, especially for forming priests, he may rightly be considered your College's Patron;
indeed, this praiseworthy Institution still accepts priests and
candidates to the priesthood today, supporting them in their
commitment to theological, spiritual, and pastoral training.

On returning to your original communities or accompanying your compatriots who have emigrated, may you be able
to inspire in each one love for God and for the Church, following the example of St. Justin De Jacobis. He crowned his fruitful contribution to the religious and civil life of the Abyssinian
peoples with the gift of his life, silently given back to God after
much suffering and persecution. He was beatified by Venerable
Pius XII on June 25, 1939, and canonized by the Servant of God
Paul VI on October 26, 1975.

Dear priests and seminarians, the way of holiness is marked
out for you, too! Christ continues to be present in the world and
to reveal himself through those who, like St. Justin De Jacobis,
allow themselves to be enlivened by his Spirit. The Second Vatican Council reminds us of this, saying, among other things,
"God shows to men, in a vivid way, his presence and his face in
the lives of those companions of ours in the human condition
who are more perfectly transformed into the image of Christ
(cf. 2 Cor 3:18), He speaks to us in them and offers us a sign of
this Kingdom."[26]

Christ, the eternal Priest of the New Covenant, who with
his special vocation to the priestly ministry has "conquered"
our life, does not suppress the characteristic qualities of the per-

26. Cf. Second Vatican Council, Dogmatic Constitution *Lumen Gentium*, no. 50.

son; on the contrary, he uplifts them, he ennobles them, and, making them his own, calls them to serve his mystery and his work. God also needs each one of us so that "in the coming ages he might show the immeasurable riches of his grace in kindness toward us in Christ Jesus" (Eph 2:7).

Despite the individual character of each one's vocation we are not separated from each other; on the contrary, we are in solidarity, in communion within a single spiritual body. We are called to form the total Christ, a unity recapitulated in the Lord, enlivened by his Spirit to become his "pleroma" and to enrich the canticle of praise that he raises to the Father.

Christ is inseparable from the Church that is his Body. It is in the Church that Christ most closely gathers around him the baptized and, nourishing them with his own Body and his Blood, makes them partakers in his own glorious life.[27]

Holiness is therefore placed in the very heart of the ecclesial mystery and is the vocation to which we are all called. The Saints are not external ornaments that adorn the Church but are like the blossom of a tree that reveals the inexhaustible vitality of the sap that rises in it. It is thus beautiful to contemplate the Church, ascending toward the fullness of the *Vir Perfectus* in continuous, demanding, and gradual maturation, dynamically impelled toward complete fulfillment in Christ.

Dear priests and seminarians of the Pontifical Ethiopian College, live with joy and dedication this important period of your formation in the shadow of the dome of St. Peter's. May you walk with determination on the path of holiness. You are a

27. Cf. Ibid., no. 48.

sign of hope, especially for the Church in your native countries. I am sure that the experience of communion you have lived here in Rome will help you also to make a precious contribution to the growth and peaceful coexistence of your beloved nations.

I accompany your progress with my prayers, and, through the intercession of St. Justin De Jacobis and of the Virgin Mary, I impart to you with affection the Apostolic Blessing that I gladly extend to the Sisters of Maria Bambina, to the Personnel of the House, and to all your loved ones.

37. What Is the Seminary For?

From *Address of His Holiness Benedict XVI,*
Meeting with Seminarians, Apostolic Journey to Germany,
September 24, 2011

It is a great joy for me to be able to come together here with young people who are setting out to serve the Lord, young people who want to listen to his call and follow him. I would like to express particularly warm thanks for the beautiful letter that the Rector and the seminarians wrote to me. It truly touched my heart to see how you had reflected on my letter and developed your own questions and answers from it, and to see how seriously you are taking what I tried to say in my letter, on the basis of which you are now working out your own path.

Of course it would be wonderful if we could hold a conversation with one another, but my travel schedule, which I am bound to follow, sadly does not permit such things. So I can only try, in the light of what you have written and what I myself had written, to offer just one or two further ideas.

In considering the questions—What is the seminary for? What does this time mean?—I am always particularly struck by the account that Saint Mark gives of the birth of the apostolic community in the third chapter of his Gospel. Mark says, "And he appointed twelve." He makes something, he does something, it is a creative act; and he made them, "to be with him, and to be sent out to preach" (Mk 12:14). That is a twofold purpose, which in many respects seems contradictory. "To be with him": they are to be with him, in order to come to know him, to hear what he says, to be formed by him; they are to go with him, to accompany him on his path, surrounding him, and following him. But at the same time they are to be envoys who go out, who take with them what they have learned, who bring it to others who are also on a journey—into the margins, into the wide open spaces, even into places far removed from him. And yet this paradox holds together: if they are truly with him, then they are also always journeying toward others, they are searching for the lost sheep; they go out, they must pass on what they have found, they must make it known, they must become envoys. And conversely, if they want to be good envoys, then they must always be with him. As Saint Bonaventure once said, the angels, wherever they go, however far away, always move within the inner being of God. This is also the case here: as priests we must go out onto the many different streets, where we find people whom we should invite to his wedding feast. But we can only do this if in the process we always remain with him. And learning this: this combination of, on the one hand, going out on mission, and on the other hand, being with him, remaining with him, is—I believe—precisely what we have to learn in the seminary. The right way of remaining with him, becoming deeply rooted in him—being more and more with him, knowing him more and more, being more and more inseparable from him—and at the same time going out more and more, bringing the message, passing it on, not keeping it to ourselves, but bringing the word to those who are far away and who nevertheless, as God's creatures and as people loved by Christ, all have a longing for him in their hearts.

The seminary is therefore a time for training; also, of course, a time for discernment, for learning: does he want me for this? The mission must be tested, and this includes being in community with others and also of course speaking with your spiritual directors, in order to learn how to discern what his will is. And then learning to trust: if he truly wants this, then I may entrust myself to him. In today's world, which is changing in such an unprecedented way and in which everything is in a constant state of flux, in which human ties are breaking down because of new encounters, it is becoming more and more difficult to believe that I will hold firm for the whole of my life. Even for my own generation, it was not exactly easy to imagine how many decades God might assign to me, and how different the world might become. Will I be able to hold firm with him, as I have promised to do? ... It is a question that demands the testing of the vocation, but then also—the more I recognize that he does indeed want me—it demands trust: if he wants me, then he will also hold me, he will be there in the hour of temptation, in the hour of need, and he will send people to me, he will show me the path, he will hold me. And faithfulness is possible, because he is always there, because he is yesterday, today, and tomorrow, because he belongs not only to this time, but he is the future and he can support us at all times.

A time for discernment, a time for learning, a time for vocation ... and then, naturally, a time for being with him, a time for praying, for listening to him. Listening, truly learning to listen to him—in the word of sacred Scripture, in the faith of the Church, in the liturgy of the Church—and learning to understand the present time in his word. In exegesis we learn much about the past: what happened, what sources there are, what communities there were, and so on. This is also important. But more important still is that from the past we should learn about the present, we should learn that he is speaking these words now, and that they all carry their present within them, and that over and above the historical circumstances in which they arose, they contain a fullness that speaks to all times. And it is important to learn this present-day aspect of his word—to learn to listen out for it—and thus to be able to speak of it to others. Naturally, when one is preparing the homily for Sunday, it often seems ... my goodness, so remote! But if I live with the word, then I see that it is not at all remote, it is highly contemporary, it is right here, it concerns me, and it concerns others. And then I also learn how to explain it. But for this, a constant inner journey with the word of God is needed.

Personally being with Christ, with the living God, is one thing: another is that we can only ever believe within the "we." I sometimes say that Saint Paul wrote, "Faith comes from hearing"—not from reading. It needs reading as well, but it comes from hearing, that is to say, from the living word, addressed to me by the other, whom I can hear, addressed to me by the

Church throughout the ages, from her contemporary word, spoken to me by the priests, bishops, and my fellow believers. Faith must include a "you," and it must include a "we." And it is very important to practice this mutual support, to learn how to accept the other as the other in his otherness, and to learn that he has to support me in my otherness, in order to become "we," so that we can also build community in the parish, calling people into the community of the word, and journeying with one another toward the living God. This requires the very particular "we" that is the seminary, and also the parish, but it also requires us always to look beyond the particular, limited "we" toward the great "we" that is the Church of all times and places: it requires that we do not make ourselves the sole criterion. When we say, "We are Church"—well, it is true: that is what we are, we are not just anybody. But the "we" is more extensive than the group that asserts those words. The "we" is the whole community of believers, today and in all times and places. And so I always say, within the community of believers, yes, there is as it were the voice of the valid majority, but there can never be a majority against the apostles or against the saints: that would be a false majority. We are Church: let us be Church, let us be Church precisely by opening ourselves and stepping outside ourselves and being Church with others.

Well, now, according to the schedule, I daresay I ought really to draw to a close now. I would like to make just one more point to you. In preparing for the priesthood, study is very much a part of the journey. This is not an academic accident that has arisen in the Western Church, it is something essential. We all know that Saint Peter said, "Always be prepared to make a defense to anyone who calls you to account for the hope that is in you" (1 Pt 3:15). Our world today is a rationalist and thoroughly scientific world, albeit often somewhat pseudo-scientific. But this scientific spirit, this spirit of understanding, explaining, know-how, rejection of the irrational, is dominant in our time. There is a good side to this, even if it often conceals much arrogance and nonsense. The faith is not a parallel world of feelings that we can still afford to hold on to, rather it is the key that encompasses everything, gives it meaning, interprets it, and also provides its inner ethical orientation: making clear that it is to be understood and lived as tending toward God and proceeding from God. Therefore it is important to be informed and to understand, to have an open mind, to learn. Naturally in twenty years' time, some quite different philosophical theories will be fashionable from those of today: when I think what counted as the highest, most modern philosophical fashion in our day, and how totally forgotten it is now ... still, learning these things is not in vain, for there will be some enduring insights among them. And most of all, this is how we learn to judge, to think through an idea—and to do so critically—and to ensure that in this thinking the light of God will serve to enlighten us and will not be extinguished. Studying is essential: only thus can we stand firm in these times and proclaim within them the reason for our faith. And it is essential that we study critically—because we know that tomorrow someone else will have something else to say—while being alert, open, and humble as we study, so that our studying is always with the Lord, before the Lord, and for him.

Yes, I could say much more, and perhaps I should ... but I thank you for your attention. In my prayers, all the seminarians of the world are present in my heart—and not only those known to me by name, like the individuals I had the pleasure of receiving here this evening; I pray, as they make their inner journey toward the Lord, that he may bless them all, give light to them all, and show them the right way, and that he may grant us to receive many good priests. Thank you very much.

38. *Education to a Solid Spiritual Life*

From *Address of His Holiness Benedict XVI to Teachers and Students of the Almo Collegio Capranica,* Clementine Hall, January 20, 2012

It always gives me joy to meet the community of the Almo Collegio Capranica, which has been one of the seminaries of the Diocese of Rome for more than five centuries. I greet with affection all of you and of course, in particular, His Eminence Cardinal Martino and the Rector, Mons. Ermenegildo Manicardi. And I thank His Eminence for his courteous words. On the occasion of the Feast of St. Agnes, Patroness of the College, I would like to offer you a few thoughts that her status suggests.

St. Agnes is one of the famous Roman maidens who demonstrated the genuine beauty of faith in Christ and of friendship with him. Her double description as Virgin and Martyr refers to the totality of the dimensions of holiness that is also required of you by your Christian faith and by the special vocation to the priesthood with which the Lord has called you to bind yourselves to him.

Martyrdom—for St. Agnes—meant generously and freely accepting to spend her young life totally and without reserve to

237

ensure that the Gospel was proclaimed as the truth and beauty that illuminate existence. In Agnes's martyrdom, which she courageously embraced in the Stadium of Domitian, the beauty of belonging to Christ without hesitation and of entrusting ourselves to him shines out forever.

Still today, for anyone strolling in Piazza Navona, the Saint's statue, high up on the pediment of the Church of Sant'Agnese in Agone, reminds us that this City of ours is also founded on friendship with Christ and on the witness to his Gospel borne by many of his sons and daughters. The generous gift of themselves to him and for the good of their brethren is a basic component of Rome's spiritual features.

Agnes also sealed in martyrdom the other crucial element of her life, *virginity* for Christ and for the Church. Indeed, the conscious, free, and mature choice of virginity testifies to the wish to belong totally to Christ and paves the way to the total gift of self in martyrdom. If martyrdom is a heroic final act, virginity is the result of a long friendship with Jesus, developed in constant listening to his word, in the dialogue of prayer, in the Eucharistic encounter.

While she was a young girl Agnes had learned that being disciples of the Lord means expressing love for him, staking one's whole life on him. Her dual status—Virgin and Martyr—reminds us that a credible witness to faith must be a person who lives for Christ, with Christ, and in Christ, transforming his or her life in accordance with the loftiest requirements of giving freely.

The priest's formation also demands wholeness, completeness, the practice of asceticism, perseverance, and heroic fidelity

THE MEANING OF SEMINARY FORMATION

in all its constituent aspects; it must be based on a solid spiritual life enlivened by an intense relationship with God at a personal and community level, with special attention in liturgical celebrations and the reception of the sacraments. Priestly life calls for a growing yearning for holiness, a clear *sensus Ecclesiae* [sense of Church], and an openness to brotherhood without exclusion or partiality.

The priest's journey to holiness also depends upon his decision to work out, with God's help, his own knowledge and commitment, a true and sound personal culture that is the product of enthusiastic and constant study. Faith has a rational and intellectual dimension of its own that is essential to it. For a seminarian and for a young priest still grappling with academic studies, it is a matter of assimilating that synthesis of faith and reason that is proper to Christianity. The Word of God became flesh, and the presbyter, a true priest of the Incarnate Word, must become, increasingly, a luminous and profound transparency of the eternal Word who was given to us.

Those who are also mature in their overall cultural formation can more effectively become teachers and animators of that adoration "in Spirit and truth" of which Jesus spoke to the Samaritan woman (cf. Jn 4:23).

This adoration that is formed through listening to the Word of God and through the power of the Holy Spirit is called, especially in the Liturgy, to become the *"rationabile obsequium"* of which the Apostle Paul speaks to us, a form of worship in which man himself, in his totality as a being endowed with reason, becomes adoration, a glorification of the living God, a worship that cannot be attained by conforming to this world, but by letting himself be transformed by Christ, renewing his way of thinking in order to discern the will of God, "what is good, acceptable and perfect" (cf. Rom 12:1-2).

Dear students of the Capranica College, your commitment in the journey to holiness, with a solid cultural training, corresponds with the original intention of this Institute, founded 555 years ago by Cardinal Domenico Capranica. May you always have a profound sense of the history and tradition of the Church! The fact that you are in Rome is a gift that must make you particularly sensitive to the depth of Catholic tradition. You already feel this tangibly in the history of the building that hosts you. In addition, you are living these years of formation especially close to the Successor of Peter: this enables you to perceive with special clarity the Church's universal dimension and the desire for the Gospel to reach all peoples.

Here you have the possibility of broadening your horizons with international experiences; here, especially, you breathe catholicity. Make the most of what you are offered for the future service of the Diocese of Rome or of the Dioceses you come from! From the friendship that will arise from community life, learn to recognize the diverse situations of the nations and Churches in the world so as to form a catholic vision. Prepare yourselves to be close to every person you meet, letting no culture be a barrier to the Word of life of which you are heralds also with your own lives.

Dear friends, the Church has great expectations of young priests in the work of evangelization and of the New Evangelization. I encourage you so that in your daily labor, rooted in the beauty of the authentic Tradition and deeply united with Christ, you may be able to bring it to your communities with truth and joy.

With the intercession of the Virgin and Martyr, Agnes, and of Mary Most Holy, Star of Evangelization, may you work to enhance the fruitfulness of your ministry. I warmly impart to you and to your loved ones the Apostolic Blessing. Many thanks.

39. *Theology and Prayer*

From *Address of His Holiness Benedict XVI to Rectors, Professors, and Seminarians of the Pontifical Seminaries of Campania, Calabria, and Umbria*, January 26, 2012

I am very pleased to receive you on the occasion of the centenary of the foundation of the Pontifical Seminaries of Campania, Calabria, and Umbria. I greet my brothers in the Episcopate and in the Priesthood, the three rectors, together with the co-workers and teachers, and I greet you especially with affection, dear seminarians! The birth of these three regional seminaries in 1912 should be seen as part of the broader task of improving the qualifications of candidates to the priesthood that was undertaken by St. Pius X, in continuity with Leo XIII.

To meet the need for a higher standard of formation, diocesan seminaries were grouped together in new regional seminaries and theological studies were streamlined. This gave rise to a tangible improvement in quality, thanks to the acquisition of a basic culture common to all and to a sufficiently long and well-structured study period. In this regard the Society of Jesus played an important role. Indeed the direction of five regional seminaries, including that in Catanzaro, was entrusted to the Jesuits from 1926 to 1941, and the one in Posillipo since its foundation to this day. However, it was not only academic formation that benefited, since the promotion of community life among young seminarians from different diocesan situations laid the foundations for considerable human enrichment. The case of the Campano Seminary in Posillipo is unique. It has been open to all the southern regions since 1935, when it was granted the faculty to award academic qualifications.

The experience of the regional seminaries is still timely and effective in the current historical and ecclesial context. Thanks to their connection with the theological faculties and institutes, they give access to higher studies, providing an appropriate training for the complex cultural and social situation in which we live. Moreover, the interdiocesan character of these seminaries is turning out to be an efficient "training ground" for communion, which is developed in the encounter of different sensibilities to be harmonized in the one service to Christ's Church.

In this regard the regional seminaries make an effective and practical contribution to the Dioceses' journey in communion to fostering knowledge, the capacity for cooperation, and an enrichment in ecclesial experiences among the future priests, the formation staff, and the Pastors of the particular Churches. The regional dimension is also an effective mediation between the line of the universal Church and the demands of the local realities that steers clear of the risk of particularism.

Your regions, dear friends, have each a rich spiritual and cultural patrimony, while they are beset by social problems. Let us think, for example, of Umbria, the homeland of St. Francis and St. Benedict! Imbued with spirituality, Umbria is a continuous pilgrimage destination. At the same time, this small region is suffering from the unfavorable economic situation as much as and more than others. In Campania and in Calabria, the vitality of the local Church, nourished by a religious sense that is still alive, thanks to solid traditions and devotions, must be expressed in a renewed evangelization. In those lands the testimony of ecclesial communities has to reckon with serious social and cultural emergencies, such as unemployment, especially for youth, and the phenomenon of organized crime.

Today's cultural context demands that priests have a solid training in philosophy and theology. As I wrote in my *Letter to Seminarians*, at the end of the Year for Priests, "the point is not simply to learn evidently useful things, but to understand and appreciate the internal structure of the faith as a whole, which is not a summary of a thesis, but an organism, an organic vision, so that it can become a response to people's questions, which on the surface change from one generation to another yet ultimately remain the same."[28]

In addition, the study of theology must always be closely tied to the life of prayer. It is important that the seminarian understand properly that while he is applying himself to this subject, it is in fact a "Subject" who is calling him, the Lord, who has enabled him to hear his voice, inviting him to spend his life at the service of God and of his brethren. Thus, in today's seminarian and tomorrow's priest, the *unity of life*, as intended by the Conciliar Document *Presbyterorum Ordinis*,[29] can be vis-

28. Pope Benedict XVI, *Letter to Seminarians*, no. 5.
29. Cf. Second Vatican Council, Decree *Presbyterorum Ordinis*, no. 14.

THE MEANING OF SEMINARY FORMATION

ibly expressed through his *pastoral charity*, "the internal principle, the force which animates and guides the spiritual life of the priest inasmuch as he is configured to Christ the Head and Shepherd."[30]

In fact the harmonious integration between the ministry, with its multiple activities, and the priest's spiritual life is indispensable. "It is important for the priest, who is called to accompany others through the journey of life up to the threshold of death, to have the right balance of heart and mind, reason and feeling, body and soul, and to be humanly integrated."[31]

These are the reasons that impel us to pay great attention to the human dimension of the formation of candidates for the priesthood. It is indeed in our humanity that we present ourselves to God, to be authentic *men of God* for our brothers. Indeed, anyone who wishes to become a priest must be first and foremost a "man of God," as St. Paul wrote to his pupil Timothy (1 Tm 6:11).... "It follows that the most important thing in our path towards priesthood and during the whole of our priestly lives is our personal relationship with God in Jesus Christ."[32]

Blessed Pope John XXIII, receiving the Superiors and students of the Campano Seminary on the occasion of the fifth anniversary of its foundation, on the eve of the Second Vatican Council, expressed this firm conviction: "Your education strives for this, in expectation of the mission that will be entrusted to you for the glory of God and the salvation of souls: to train the mind, to sanctify the will. The world is waiting for saints; this

30. Pope John Paul II, Apostolic Exhortation *Pastores Dabo Vobis*, no. 23.
31. Pope Benedict XVI, *Letter to Seminarians*, October 18, 2010, no. 6.
32. Ibid., no. 1.

above all. We need holy and sanctifying priests even more than cultured, eloquent and up-to-date priests."[33]

These words still sound timely because—throughout the Church, and in your specific regions of origin—the need for Gospel workers, credible witnesses, and those who champion holiness with their own lives is more pressing than ever. May each one of you respond to this call! I assure you of my prayer for this, while I entrust you to the motherly guidance of the Blessed Virgin Mary and warmly impart to you a special Apostolic Blessing.

33. Pope John XXIII, Address to Extraordinary Diplomatic Missions Representing Their Governments at the Solemn Opening of the II Vatican Ecumenical Council (October 12, 1962).

CONCLUSION

The Future Belongs to Us

From *Lectio Divina of the Holy Father,* Pontifical Major
Roman Seminary, February 8, 2013

Every year it gives me great joy to be here with you and to see so many young men bound for the priesthood who are attentive to the Lord's voice, who want to follow this voice and seek the way to serve the Lord in our time.

We have heard three verses from the First Letter of St. Peter (cf. 1 Pt 1:3–5). Before going into this text it seems to me important to be aware of the fact that it is Peter who is speaking. The first two words of the Letter are *"Petrus apostolus"* (cf. 1 Pt 1:1): he speaks, and he speaks to the Churches in Asia and calls the faithful "chosen" and "exiles of the Dispersion" (1 Pt 1:1). Let us reflect a little on this. Peter is speaking, and—as we hear at the end of the Letter—he is speaking from Rome, which he called "Babylon" (cf. 1 Pt 5:13). Peter speaks as if it were a first encyclical with which the first Apostle, Vicar of Christ, addresses the Church of all time.

Peter, an apostle: thus the one who is speaking is the one who found the Messiah in Jesus Christ, who was the first to speak on behalf of the future Church: "You are the Christ, the Son of the living God" (cf. Mt 16:16). The one who introduced

247

us to this faith is speaking, the one to whom the Lord said, "I will give you the keys of the kingdom of heaven" (cf. Mt 16:19), to whom he entrusted his flock after the Resurrection, saying to him three times, "Feed my lambs.... Tend my sheep" (cf. Jn 21:15–17). And it is also the man who fell who is speaking, the man who denied Jesus three times and was granted the grace to see Jesus' look, to feel deeply moved in his heart and to find forgiveness and a renewal of his mission. However, above all it is important that this man, full of passion, full of longing for God, full of a desire for the Kingdom of God, for the Messiah, this man who has found Jesus, the Lord and the Messiah, is also the man who sinned, who fell; and yet he remained in God's sight, and in this way he remained responsible for the Lord's Church, he remained the one assigned by Christ, he remained the messenger of Christ's love.

Peter the Apostle is speaking, but the exegetes tell us it is impossible for this Letter to have been written by Peter because the Greek is so good that it cannot be the Greek of a fisherman from the Sea of Galilee. And it is not only the language—the syntax is excellent—but also the thought that is already quite mature, there are actual formulas in which the faith and the reflection of the Church are summed up. These exegetes say, therefore, it had already reached a degree of development that cannot be Peter's. How does one respond? There are two important positions: first, Peter himself—that is, the Letter—gives us a clue, for at the end of the writing he says, I write to you "by Silvanus ... *dia* Silvanus" (1 Pt 5:12). This "by" (*dia*) could mean various things. It may mean that he (Silvanus) brings or transmits; it may mean that Silvanus helped him write it; it may mean that in practice it was really Silvanus who wrote it. In any case, we may conclude that the Letter itself points out to us that Peter was not alone in writing this Letter, but that it expresses the faith of a Church, which is already on a journey of faith, a faith increasingly mature. He does not write alone, as an isolated individual; he writes with the assistance of the Church, of people who help him to deepen the faith, to enter into the depths of his thought, of his rationality, of his profundity. And this is very important: Peter is not speaking as an individual, he is speaking *ex persona Ecclesiae*, he is speaking as a man of the Church, as an individual, of course, with his personal responsibility, but also as a person who speaks on behalf of the Church; not only private and original ideas, not as a nineteenth-century genius who wished to express only personal and original ideas that no one else could have expressed first. No. He does not speak as an individualistic genius, but speaks, precisely, in the communion of the Church. In the Apocalypse, in the initial vision of Christ, it is said that Christ's voice is like the sound of many waters (cf. Rv 1:15). This means: Christ's voice gathers together all the waters of the world, bears within it all the living waters that give life to the world; he is a Person, but this is the very greatness of the Lord, that he bears within him all the rivers of the Old Testament, indeed, of the wisdom of peoples. And what is said of the Lord also applies here, in a different way, to the Apostle. This does not mean to say a word that is his alone, but one that really contains the waters of faith, the waters of the whole Church, and in this very way gives fertility, gives fecundity. Thus it is a personal witness that is open to the Lord and thereby becomes open and broad. So this is very important.

249

Then I think it is important that in the conclusion of the Letter Silvanus and Mark are mentioned, two people who were also friends of St. Paul. So it is that through this conclusion the worlds of St. Peter and St. Paul converge: there is no exclusive Petrine theology as against a Pauline theology, but a theology of the Church, of the faith of the Church, in which there is— of course—a diversity of temperament, of thought, of style, between the manner of speaking of Paul and that of Peter. It is right that these differences should also exist today. There are different charisms, different temperaments, yet they are not in conflict but are united in the common faith.

I would like to say something more: St. Peter writes from Rome. This is important. Here we already have the Bishop of Rome, we have the beginning of Succession, we already have the beginning of the actual Primacy located in Rome, not only granted by the Lord but placed here, in this city, in this world capital. How did Peter come to Rome? This is a serious question. The Acts of the Apostles tell us that after his escape from Herod's prison, he went to another place (cf. Acts 12:17)—*eis eteron topon*—where he went is not known; some say to Antioch, others, to Rome. In any case, in this capital it should also be said that before fleeing he entrusted the Judeo-Christian Church, the Church of Jerusalem, to James, and in entrusting her to James he nevertheless remained Primate of the universal Church, of the Church of the Gentiles but also of the Judeo-Christian Church. And here in Rome he found a great Judeo-Christian community. The liturgists tell us that in the Roman Canon there are traces of a characteristically Judeo-Christian language. Thus we see that in Rome both parts of the Church were to be found: the

Judeo-Christian and the pagan-Christian, united, an expression of the universal Church. And for Peter, moving from Jerusalem to Rome meant moving to the universality of the Church, moving to the Church of the Gentiles and of all the epochs, to the Church that also still belongs to the Jews. And I think that in going to Rome St. Peter not only thought of this transfer: Jerusalem / Rome, Judeo-Christian Church / universal Church. He certainly also remembered Jesus' last words to him, recorded by St. John: "when you are old, you will stretch out your hands, and another will gird you and carry you where you do not wish to go" (cf. Jn 21:18). It is a prophecy of the crucifixion. Philologists show us that "stretch out your hands" is a precise, technical expression for the crucifixion. St. Peter knew that his end would be martyrdom, would be the cross: that it would therefore be following Christ completely. Consequently, in going to Rome there is no doubt that he was also going to martyrdom: martyrdom awaited him in Babylon. The primacy, therefore, has this content of universality, but it has a martyrological content, as well. Furthermore, Rome had been a place of martyrdom from the outset. In going to Rome, Peter once again accepts this word of the Lord: he heads for the cross and invites us too to accept the martyrological aspect of Christianity, which may have very different forms. And the cross may have very different forms, but no one can be Christian without following the Crucified One, without accepting the martyrological moment, too.

After these words about the author, a brief word too about the people to whom the Letter was written. I have already said that St. Peter describes those to whom he wrote with the words *"eklektois parepidemois,"* "to the chosen who are exiles of the Dispersion" (cf. 1 Pt 1:1). Once again we have this paradox of glory and of the cross: chosen, but exiles and foreigners. *Chosen*: this was Israel's title of glory: we are the chosen ones, God chose this small people not because it was more in number—Deuteronomy says—but because he loves it (cf. Dt 7:7–8). We are *chosen*: St. Peter now transfers this to all the baptized, and the very content of the first chapters of his First Letter is that the baptized are admitted to the privileges of Israel, they are the new Israel. *Chosen*: I think it is worth reflecting on this word. We are *chosen*. God has always known us, even before our birth, before our conception; God wanted me as a Christian, as a Catholic, he wanted me as a priest. God thought of me, he sought me among millions, among a great many, he saw me and he chose me. It was not for my merits, which were nonexistent, but out of his goodness; he wanted me to be a messenger of his choice, which is also always a mission, above all a mission, and a responsibility for others. *Chosen*: we must be grateful and joyful for this event. God thought of me, he chose me as a Catholic, me, as a messenger of his Gospel, as a priest. In my opinion it is worth reflecting several times on this and coming back to this fact of his choice; he chose me, he wanted me; now I am responding.

Perhaps today we are tempted to say we do not want to rejoice at having been chosen, for this would be triumphalism. It would be triumphalism to think that God had chosen me because I was so important. This would really be erroneous triumphalism. However, being glad because God wanted me is not triumphalism. Rather, it is gratitude, and I think we should relearn this joy: God wanted me to be born in this way, into a Catholic family, he wanted me to know Jesus from the first.

What a gift to be wanted by God so that I could know his face, so that I could know Jesus Christ, the human face of God, the human history of God in this world! Being joyful because he has chosen me to be a Catholic, to be in this Church of his, where *subsistit Ecclesia unica*; we should rejoice because God has given me this grace, this beauty of knowing the fullness of God's truth, the joy of his love.

Chosen: a word of privilege and at the same time of humility. However, "chosen"—as I said—is accompanied by the word *"parepidemois,"* exiles, foreigners. As Christians we are dispersed and we are foreigners: we see that Christians are the most persecuted group in the world today, because it does not conform, because it is a stimulus, because it opposes the tendencies to selfishness, to materialism, and to all these things.

Christians are certainly not only foreigners; we are also Christian nations, we are proud of having contributed to the formation of culture; there is a healthy patriotism, a healthy joy of belonging to a nation that has a great history of culture and of faith. Yet, as Christians, we are always also foreigners—the destiny of Abraham, described in the Letter to the Hebrews. As Christians we are, even today, also always foreigners. In the workplace Christians are a minority, they find themselves in an extraneous situation; it is surprising that a person today can still believe and live like this. This is also part of our life: it is a form of being with the Crucified Christ; this being foreigners, not living in the way that everyone else lives, but living—or at least seeking to live—in accordance with his Word, very differently from what everyone says. And it is precisely this that is characteristic of Christians. They all say, "But everyone does this, why don't I?" No, I don't, because I want to live in accordance with God. St Augustine once said, Christians are those who do not have their roots below, like trees, but have their roots above, and they do not live this gravity in the natural downward gravitation. Let us pray the Lord that he help us to accept this mission of living as exiles, as a minority, in a certain sense, of living as foreigners and yet being responsible for others and, in this way, reinforcing the goodness in our world.

Lastly let us come to the three verses of today. I would only like to stress or, let us say, briefly interpret, as far as I can, three terms: the term "born anew," the term "inheritance," and the term "guarded through faith." *Born anew—anaghennesas*, the Greek text says—means that being Christian is not merely a decision of my will, an idea of mine; I see there is a group I like, I join this group, I share their aims, etc. No. Being Christian does not mean entering a group to do something, it is not only an act of my will, not primarily of my will, of my reason. It is an act of God. *Born anew* does not solely concern the sphere of the will or of thought, but the sphere of being. I am reborn: this means that becoming Christian is first of all passive; I cannot make myself Christian, but I am caused to be reborn, I am remade by the Lord in the depths of my being. And I enter into this process of rebirth, I let myself be transformed, renewed, reborn. This seems to me very important: as a Christian I do not just form an idea of my own that I share with a few others, and if I do not like them anymore I can leave. No: it concerns the very depths of being, namely, becoming a Christian begins with an action of God, above all with an action of his, and I let myself be formed and transformed.

CONCLUSION

I think that a topic for reflection, especially in a year in which
we are reflecting on the sacraments of Christian Initiation, is the
meditation on this: this passive and active depth of being born
anew, of becoming one with Christian life, of letting myself be
transformed by his Word, for the communion of the Church, for
the life of the Church, for the signs with which the Lord works
in me, works with me and for me. And being reborn, being born
anew, also means that I thereby enter a new family: God, my
Father, the Church, my mother, other Christians, my brothers
and sisters. Being born anew, letting ourselves be born anew,
therefore involves deliberately letting ourselves be incorporated into this family, living for God the Father and by God the
Father, living by communion with Christ his Son who causes
me to be born anew through his Resurrection, as the Letter says
(cf. 1 Pt 1:3), living with the Church, letting myself be formed by
the Church in so many ways, in so many processes, and being
open to my brethren, really recognizing others as my brothers
and sisters, who are born anew with me, transformed, renewed;
each is responsible for the other, hence a responsibility of Baptism that is a lifelong process of the whole of life.

The second term: *inheritance*. It is a very important word in
the Old Testament, where Abraham is told that his seed will inherit the earth, and this was always the promise for his descendants. You will have the earth, you will be heirs of the earth.
In the New Testament, this word becomes a word for us; we
are *heirs*, not of a specific country, but of the land of God, of the
future of God. Inheritance is something of the future, and thus
this word tells us above all that as Christians we have a future,
the future is ours, the future is God's. Thus, being Christians,

255

we know that the future is ours, and the tree of the Church is not a tree that is dying but a tree that constantly puts out new shoots. Therefore we have a reason not to let ourselves be upset, as Pope John said, by the prophets of doom who say, well, the Church is a tree that grew from the mustard seed, grew for two thousand years, now she has time behind her, it is now time for her to die. No. The Church is ever renewed, she is always reborn. The future belongs to us. Of course, there is a false optimism and a false pessimism. A false pessimism tells us that the epoch of Christianity is over. No: it is beginning again! The false optimism was the post-Council optimism, when convents closed, seminaries closed, and they said, "but ... nothing, everything is fine!" ... No! Everything is not fine. There are also serious, dangerous omissions, and we have to recognize with healthy realism that in this way things are not all right, it is not all right when errors are made. However, we must also be certain at the same time that if, here and there, the Church is dying because of the sins of men and women, because of their nonbelief, at the same time she is reborn. The future really belongs to God: this is the great certainty of our life, the great, true optimism that we know. The Church is the tree of God that lives forever and bears within her eternity and the true inheritance: eternal life.

And, lastly, "guarded through faith." The New Testament text, from the Letter of St. Peter, uses a rare word here, *phrouroumenoi*, which means, there are the "guards," and faith is like the guards who preserve the integrity of my being, of my faith. This word interprets in particular "the guards" at the gates of a city, where they stand and keep watch over the city so that it is not invaded by destructive powers. Thus faith is a "guard" of my being, of my life, of my inheritance. We must be grateful for this vigilance of faith that protects us, helps us, guides us, gives us the security: God does not let me fall from his hands: *Safeguarded by faith*: I'll end with this. Speaking of faith I must always think of that sick woman among the crowd who, gaining access to Jesus, touched him in order to be healed and was healed. The Lord said, "Who touched my garments?" They said to him, "You see the crowd pressing around you, and yet you say, 'who touched me?'" (cf. Mk 5:–52-34, 7:27–30). But the Lord knows there is a way of touching him that is superficial, external, that really has nothing to do with a true encounter with him. And there is a way of touching him profoundly. And this woman truly touched him: she did not only touch him with her hand, but with her heart and thus received Christ's healing power, truly touching him from within, from faith. This is faith: touching Christ with the hand of faith, with our heart, and thus entering into the power of his life, into the healing power of the Lord. And let us pray the Lord that we may touch him more and more, so as to be healed. Let us pray that he will not let us fall, that he too may take us by the hand and thus preserve us for true life. Many thanks.

INDEX

259

INDEX

INDEX

Called to Holiness: On Love, Vocation, and Formation was designed and typeset in Dante by Kachergis Book Design of Pittsboro, North Carolina. It was printed on 60-pound Natural Recycled and bound by McNaughton & Gunn of Saline, Michigan.